The Stamp Chronicles

OrangeBooks Publication

Smriti Nagar, Bhilai, Chhattisgarh - 490020

Website: **www.orangebooks.in**

First Edition, 2023

The Stamp Chronicles

A Journey Through Philately

OrangeBooks Publication

www.orangebooks.in

"Not Philosophers, But
Fret - Sawyers and Stamp Collectors Compose The
Back Bone of Society."

Aldous Huxley

Foreword

The postage stamps, though small in size, have a supernatural ability to transcend time and geography. They are silent messengers of stories, traditions, and revolutions.

The journey you are about to undertake offers more than just knowledge; it offers a sense of connection to the world and to history itself.

This book is not just for collectors; it's for anyone who has ever been interested in the power of a postage stamp to tell a story, to commemorate a significant event. It's for those who appreciate the artistry that can be contained in a square inch of paper and the curiosity that drives us to seek out the stories behind these miniature treasures.

As you dive into **"The Stamp Chronicles,"** I encourage you to approach it not as a mere book but as a gateway to a world that will broaden your horizons, ignite your curiosity, and kindle a lifelong passion for philately. Whether you are an experienced collector or a newcomer to the philately, this journey promises to be an unforgettable one.

So, dear reader, fasten your seatbelt and prepare to embark on a remarkable voyage through **"The Stamp Chronicles: A Journey Through Philately."** The stamps await, and their stories are ready to be unveiled.

Happy Philatelic Journey!

Javaid Muhammad, FRPSL
Chairman
FIP Literature Commission

Introduction

In the digital age, where communication flows effortlessly through the invisible channels of the internet, it's easy to forget the tangible and timeless power of a postage stamp. Yet, within these small adhesive squares lies a world of history, culture, and human connection waiting to be discovered. Welcome to **"The Stamp Chronicles - A Journey Through Philately."**

As the founder of the Nirmala Devi Foundation, an organization dedicated to promoting education, culture, and the arts, I have had the privilege of witnessing the profound impact of stamps on our world. Philately, the study and collection of postage stamps may seem like a niche hobby, but it is an art form and a window into the past that transcends borders, languages, and generations.

This book is a labour of love and a testament to the enduring fascination that stamps hold for collectors and enthusiasts around the world. Within its pages, you will embark on a journey through time and geography, exploring the rich tapestry of human history and culture through the lens of philately.

In **"The Stamp Chronicles,"** you embark on a global voyage, as each chapter delves into the history of postage stamps, shedding light on the evolution of the postal system. From foot messengers to the high-tech delivery methods of the present day, this book provides a comprehensive exploration of the art and historical significance of postage stamps.

Moreover, **"The Stamp Chronicles"** delves into the role of philately in fostering cultural exchange and understanding, emphasizing how this hobby is important. It highlights how stamps have been used as a means of diplomacy, a platform for artistic expression, and a tool for educating the masses.

As you turn the pages of this book, I hope you will be inspired to look at stamps in a new light, recognizing their importance as more than just pieces of paper with adhesive backing. They are, in fact, windows to the world, mirrors of history, and reflections of the human spirit.

So, embark on this journey through the world of philately, and discover the stories that lie within the stamps - the tales of nations, the expressions of creativity, and the bonds that unite us all. **"The Stamp Chronicles"** invites you to join us on this remarkable expedition, where every stamp tells a story, and every collection is a testament to the enduring human desire to connect, commemorate, and communicate through the art of the postage stamp.

Gajanand Agarwal
Founder-Nirmala Devi Foundation,
Sikkim, India

About The Author

 **Roshan Prasad**, a cricket philatelist, was introduced to the stamp collection in mid-2005. Within a remarkably short span, he garnered numerous accolades for his exceptional philatelic displays on both national and international stages. His noteworthy achievements include Silver at the World Stamp Championship Exhibition, along with a remarkable 5 international-level and 5 national-level awards for his philatelic exhibits. His previous book, **"The Stamp Collector's Dictionary"**, has also won several awards at the National and International level.

He has dedicated himself to designing "Special Covers" and "Picture Post Cards" for the Department of Posts, Government of India, for the past 13 years. These exclusive editions bear significance as they commemorate individuals, places, or events of note. To his credit, he has conceived and designed an impressive assortment of 13 Special Covers and 4 Picture Post Cards, all of which have been published by the Department of Posts, Government of India.

Roshan was born to parents R.S. Prasad and Meera Devi in Singtam, Sikkim, India. He completed his schooling in Singtam and Gangtok, Sikkim, India, and later earned his Bachelor's in Commerce from the University of Calcutta, West Bengal, India.

Notably, Roshan holds the position of Treasurer for the Sikkim Philatelic Society, and his stature is further affirmed by his life membership in the Philatelic Congress of India and membership in the Emirates Philatelic Association, United Arab Emirates.

Contents

1

Stamp Collection

"The King of Hobbies"

Stamp collection, also known as philately, is a hobby people of all ages enjoy. It has been one of the world's most popular hobbies since the late nineteenth century with the rapid growth of the postal service. Referred as "The King of Hobby and the Hobby of Kings", stamp collecting is a joyful pastime that offers the philatelist (stamp collector) a chance to learn about foreign countries, their history, art, culture, religion, civilization, and language. A specialty of Stamp Collecting is that this hobby is the most democratic of all the hobbies. Nation, language, age, sex, and color do not constitute any barriers to stamp collecting. Hobbyists who collect stamps love to learn about the stories behind their stamps, as well as explore the world behind the production of stamps. Every time you collect an old stamp, you will likely be curious enough about its origin and would definitely be interested in reading up on the history of that stamp. Collecting stamps introduces history into your world, as you want to know everything related to the stamps in your collection.

It is said that Mr. John Bourke, Receiver General of Stamp Dues in Ireland, was the first collector. In 1774, he assembled a book of the existing embossed revenue stamps, ranging in value from 6 pounds to half a penny, as well as the hand-written, stamped charge marks that we used with them. Still, his collection is preserved in Dublin, Republic of Ireland.

Postage stamp collecting began at the same time when the stamps were first issued in 1840 by Sir Rowland Hill of London, Great Britain, and by 1860, thousands of collectors and stamp dealers were appearing around the world as this new study and hobby spread across Europe, European colonies, The United States and other parts of the world.

A worldwide collection of stamps would be huge, running to thousands of volumes, and would be incredibly expensive to acquire. Many collectors limit their collection to particular countries, certain time periods, or specific themes, which is pretty popular among collectors these days. Some of the popular collecting areas include Definitive stamps, Commemorative stamps, Postal stationery (includes government-issued postcards, aerograms, envelopes, etc., that have an imprinted stamp), Revenue stamps (issued to pay taxes), Postmarks, Cancellations, Franking, First Day Covers, Special Covers, Maximum cards, Miniature Sheets, Sheetlets, etc.

Children and teenagers were early collectors of stamps in the 1860s and 1870s. Many adults dismissed it as a childish pursuit, but later, many of those same collectors, as adults, began to systematically study the available postage stamps and publish books about them. In 2013, the Wall Street Journal estimated that the global number of stamp collectors was around 60 million. Tens of thousands of stamp dealers supply them with stamps along with stamp albums, catalogs, and other publications. There are also thousands of Philatelic clubs, societies, and associations that provide them with the history and other aspects of stamps. Today, though the number of stamp collectors is somewhat less as compared to a hundred years ago, stamp collecting is still one of the world's most popular indoor hobbies.

2

The History of Postage Stamps

From Communication Revolution to Collectible Art

The postage stamp, a small adhesive paper that carries the power to facilitate communication and connect individuals across vast distances, is a remarkable invention that has played a pivotal role in shaping the modern world. Its history is intertwined with technological advancements, social change, and even the evolution of art and culture. Let's take you on the fascinating journey of the postage stamp from its inception to its present-day significance as both a means of communication and a collectible art form.

Sir Rowland Hill

Inception and Evolution: The concept of a prepaid postage system dates back to ancient times, but it wasn't until the early 19th century that the idea of a postage stamp as we know it today began to take shape. In 1837, Sir Rowland Hill, a British educator and postal reformer, proposed the revolutionary idea of a uniform postage rate regardless of distance and a prepayment mechanism using adhesive labels. This concept aimed to streamline the postal system and eliminate the complexities of postage calculation based on distance and weight.

The world's first adhesive postage stamp, the Penny Black, was issued in Great Britain on May 1, 1840. Designed by Henry Corbould and featuring the profile of Queen Victoria, the Penny Black marked the beginning of a new era in communication. Its success in simplifying postage payment and reducing fraud paved the way for the global adoption of postage stamps.

Communication Revolution: The introduction of postage stamps brought about a communication revolution. Previously, the recipient of a letter was responsible for paying the postage fee upon delivery. With the implementation of prepaid stamps, the payment burden shifted to the sender, making it easier and more affordable for people to send letters and parcels. This change democratized communication, enabling people from all walks of life to exchange thoughts, news, and sentiments across great distances.

The spread of the postage stamp system was swift, with various countries adopting the concept and designing their own stamps. Each stamp often carried symbols of national identity, historical figures, or cultural motifs, reflecting the values and heritage of the issuing nation. Stamps became a microcosm of history and culture, encapsulating the spirit of their time.

Collectible and Cultural Significance: As time went on, postage stamps began to transcend their utilitarian purpose and took on an additional role as collectible items. Philately, the study and collection of stamps emerged as a passionate hobby for many enthusiasts. People were drawn to the diverse and intricate designs, historical significance, and the stories behind each stamp. Some rare stamps even gained immense monetary value, making philately not only a cultural pursuit but also an investment.

Stamps also became a canvas for art and design. As governments and postal authorities recognized the potential of stamps to convey their country's cultural heritage, they started commissioning renowned artists to create stamp designs. This practice elevated the postage stamp from a functional label to a piece of miniature art. Collectors appreciated the creativity and craftsmanship that went into each design, fostering a symbiotic relationship between philately and the world of visual arts.

Modern Significance: In the digital age, when electronic communication has largely replaced traditional mail, postage stamps might be considered obsolete. However, their significance endures. Stamps continue to be issued and serve as tangible representations of historical events, milestones, and cultural expressions. They also play a role in raising awareness for important social causes, as commemorative stamps are often issued to mark significant events or promote philanthropic efforts.

Furthermore, the world of philately remains vibrant, with stamp enthusiasts fostering communities, attending exhibitions, and preserving the legacy of postage stamps. Collectors value stamps not only for their potential investment but also for the joy of connecting with history, culture, and art.

The postage stamp stands as a testament to human ingenuity and the power of communication. From its humble beginnings as a simple adhesive label, it has evolved into a symbol of global connection, cultural representation, and artistic expression. The history of postage stamps reminds us that even in an age of instant digital communication, there is value in the tangible, the historical, and the artistic. As long as there is a desire to connect with others and appreciate the beauty of the world, the postage stamp will continue to hold its place in the tapestry of human communication and culture.

3

The World of Postage Stamps

More Than Just Paper & Ink

In an era dominated by instant communication and digital technology, the postage stamp might appear as a quaint relic of the past. However, this seemingly unassuming piece of paper carries within it a fascinating blend of history, art, culture, and practicality. Beyond its utilitarian function as evidence of postage payment, the stamp has evolved into an emblem of human ingenuity and creativity, encapsulating the stories of nations, events, and individuals.

At its core, a postage stamp is a symbol of connectivity. It represents the conduit through which letters, parcels, and sentiments navigate the globe, connecting people separated by vast distances. Before the advent of electronic communication, postage stamps played a pivotal role in uniting loved ones, conveyingimportant news, and facilitating business transactions. Each stamp encapsulated a sender's wish for their missive to safely reach its destination, often accompanied by the anticipation of a response.

However, a postage stamp is not merely a medium for conveying messages but also a canvas for artistic expression. The imagery, colors, and designs that grace these miniature works of art reflect the cultural, historical, and social identity of a nation. From iconic landmarks to national flora and fauna, from historical figures to commemorative events, stamps encapsulate the essence of a country in a tiny space. Renowned artists and designers have contributed their talents to stamp design, making these small rectangles an embodiment of visual aesthetics.

Moreover, the world of stamp collecting, known as philately, has transformed the postage stamp from a functional item into a sought-after treasure. Philatelists meticulously curate collections that span decades or even centuries, aiming to preserve a slice of history. Rare stamps, those with printing errors or limited production runs, can fetch exorbitant prices on the collectors' market. The pursuit of these tiny treasures has not only led to a thriving hobby but has also inspired a deeper understanding of history, geography, and the evolving world of printing technology.

The significance of postage stamps is not confined to their artistic and collectible aspects. They also reflect the evolving nature of postal services and technology. As postal systems modernize, so too have the stamps evolved. The traditional gummed stamp is now often accompanied by self-adhesive varieties. Digital stamps and online postage services are also changing the landscape of traditional mail. However, the essence of a postage stamp, a symbol of prepayment and validation of postal service, remains consistent, even as the methods of communication have diversified.

In conclusion, a postage stamp is not just a piece of paper with adhesive backing. It is a window into history, a canvas for artistry, a symbol of connectivity, and a testament to human creativity. It serves as a bridge between sender and recipient, embodying the hopes, emotions, and stories that travel alongside it. Whether collected as historical artifacts, cherished for their beauty, or used for their intended purpose, postage stamps continue to hold a place of intrigue and importance in our ever-changing world.

4

The Evolution of Postal Mail

From Foot Messengers to High - Tech Delivery

The transportation of postal mail has evolved significantly over the years, reflecting advancements in technology, communication, and transportation. Here's an overview of how postal mail has travelled through different historical periods:

Ancient Times and Early Civilizations: In ancient civilizations such as Egypt, Greece, and Rome, messages were often carried by messengers on foot or horseback. These messengers would travel long distances to deliver important documents or messages to various destinations.

Pigeon Post (5th Century): The use of pigeon mail or pigeon post can be traced back to ancient civilizations, including the Greeks and Persians, dating as far back as the 5th century BC. However, it became more widely practiced and organized during various historical periods, with notable instances during wartime and in remote areas where traditional postal services were lacking. It was a historical method of sending messages or small parcels using trained homing pigeons, relying on their ability to return to their home location with the message or package attached to them.

Pony Express (19th Century): In the mid-1800s, the Pony Express was a short-lived but iconic mail delivery system in the United States. Riders on horseback would cover long distances, relaying mail between Missouri and California. This service significantly reduced the time it took for mail to travel across the country.

Stagecoaches and Steamships (19th Century): During the 19th century, as transportation technology improved, stagecoaches and steamships played a crucial role in transporting mail across land and sea. These modes of transportation allowed mail to be delivered more efficiently and over longer distances.

Railroads (19ᵗʰ to 20ᵗʰ Century): The development of railroads revolutionized mail transportation. Rail networks allowed for faster and more reliable mail delivery over longer distances. Mail could be sorted and transported in bulk, leading to the establishment of railway post offices (RPOs) where mail was sorted en route.

Airmail (Early to Mid-20ᵗʰ Century): The introduction of airplanes and aviation technology opened up the possibility of faster long-distance mail delivery. Airmail services were launched in various countries, with dedicated planes flying mail routes. This significantly reduced the time it took for mail to travel internationally.

Postal Trucks and Vehicles (20th Century): With the growth of road networks and automobile technology, postal trucks and vehicles became an integral part of mail transportation. These vehicles allowed mail to be delivered to both urban and remote areas.

Digital Revolution and Electronic Communication (Late 20th Century): The rise of email and digital communication had a significant impact on the volume of physical mail being sent. As electronic communication became more prevalent, traditional postal services saw a decline in the volume of letters and paper-based correspondence.

Modern Postal Services (21ˢᵗ Century): In the present day, postal services have adapted to the changing landscape of communication. While traditional mail continues to be transported via trucks, trains, and airplanes, many postal services have expanded their offerings to include package delivery, logistics, and e-commerce solutions. Advanced tracking and tracing technologies allow both senders and recipients to monitor the progress of their mail and packages in real-time.

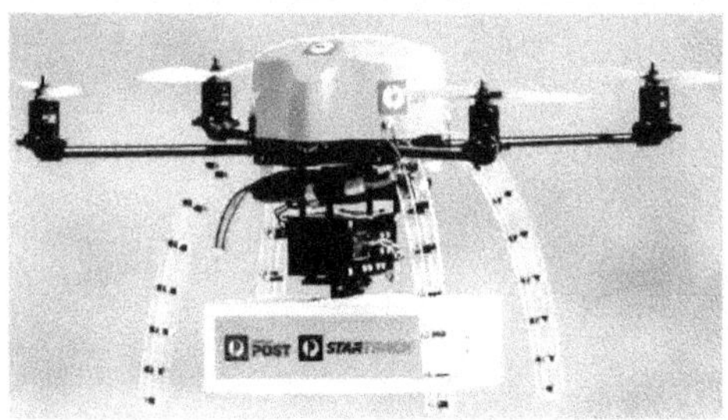

Innovations and Future Trends: The postal industry continues to evolve with the integration of technologies like automation, robotics, and artificial intelligence. Drones are being explored as a potential means of delivering mail to remote areas. Additionally, some postal services are experimenting with environmentally friendly transportation options to reduce their carbon footprint.

Overall, the journey of postal mail over the years reflects the intertwining advancements in transportation, technology, and communication, shaping how we connect and share information across vast distances.

5

How to Start Your Stamp Collection Journey

A Step-by-Step Guide

Research and Learn: Before starting to collect stamps, take some time to learn about the hobby. Read books, articles, and online resources about stamp collecting. Understanding the history of stamps, different types of stamps, and collecting terminology will give you a good foundation.

Define Your Focus: Stamp collecting is a vast hobby, and there are many ways to approach it. Decide what aspect of stamp collecting interests you the most. Some common focuses include collecting stamps from a specific country, collecting stamps on a particular theme (e.g., animals, sports, space), or collecting rare and valuable stamps. Your focus will determine the direction of your collection.

Gather Materials: You'll need some basic materials to get started, including stamp albums, magnifying glass, tweezers, and a perforation gauge. You can find these supplies at hobby shops or online stores that specialize in philatelic materials.

Start Collecting Stamps: Begin your collection by acquiring stamps. Here are some ways to get stamps:

- **Ask Friends and Family:** Let friends and family know about your new hobby, and they might give you stamps they have lying around.

- **Buy Stamps:** You can purchase stamps from local stamp dealers, online stamp shops, or at stamp shows and auctions.

- **Join a Club:** Consider joining a local stamp collecting club or online forums where collectors often trade or sell stamps.

Organize Your Stamps: As you acquire stamps, organize them in your stamp album according to your chosen focus. Catalogue and label your stamps with information such as date of issue, country, or any relevant details.

Learn About Valuation: If you're interested in collecting valuable stamps, learn how to assess the condition and rarity of stamps. There are grading systems for stamps; some stamps can be quite valuable. Be cautious when purchasing expensive stamps, and consider consulting with experienced collectors or experts.

Explore Specializations: As your collection grows, you might want to explore specific places within stamp collecting. For example, you could focus on first-day covers (envelopes with stamps cancelled on their first day of issue), postal history (covers and postmarks), or error stamps (stamps with printing mistakes).

Stay Informed: Keep up with the latest developments in the world of stamp collecting. Subscribe to philatelic magazines, follow online forums, and attend stamp shows to connect with other collectors and learn about new stamp releases.

Enjoy the Hobby: Stamp collecting should be an enjoyable and relaxing pursuit. Take your time and enjoy the process of building your collection.

It's a hobby that can be as casual or as serious as you want it to be.

Share Your Collection: Consider sharing your collection with others. You can exhibit your stamps at local stamp shows, participate in stamp club activities, or even create a website or social media account to showcase your collection to a wider audience.

Remember that stamp collecting is a hobby that can be as affordable or as expensive as you make it. Start small, enjoy the process, and gradually expand your collection based on your interests and budget. Happy collecting.

6

Essential Accessories for Collecting

Preserving, Organizing and Displaying Your Collection

Stamp collecting, also known as philately, is a popular hobby that often requires a variety of accessories to properly preserve, organize, and display your stamp collection. Here are some basic accessories commonly used by stamp collectors:

1. **Stamp Albums:** Stamp albums are books or binders with pages designed to hold and display stamps. They come in various sizes and formats, such as hingeless albums, stock books, or specialized albums for specific countries or themes.

2. **Stamp Mounts:** Stamp mounts are clear plastic or acetate holders that protect and display individual stamps. They are available in different sizes to fit various stamp dimensions and can be affixed to album pages.

3. **Magnifying Glass:** A magnifying glass with varying magnification levels is essential for examining and identifying the finer details of stamps, such as watermarks, perforations, and printing flaws.

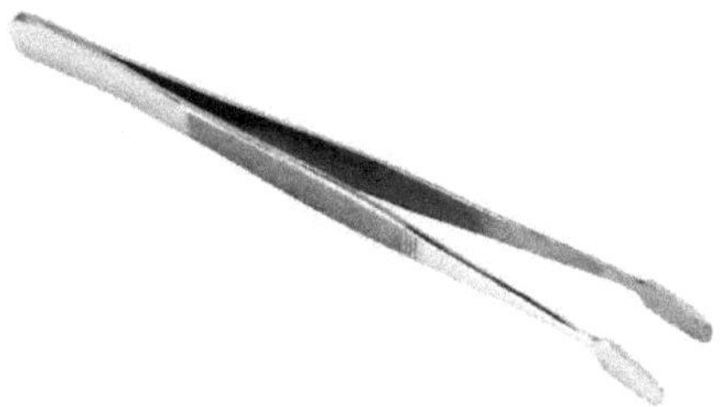

4. **Tongs or Stamp Tweezers:** Stamp tongs or tweezers are used to handle stamps without damaging them. They are typically made of plastic or metal and have pointed tips for precise handling.

5. **Watermark Detector:** A watermark detector helps identify the watermarks on stamps, which can be important for classifying and valuing them. This can be a simple tool or a more advanced electronic device.

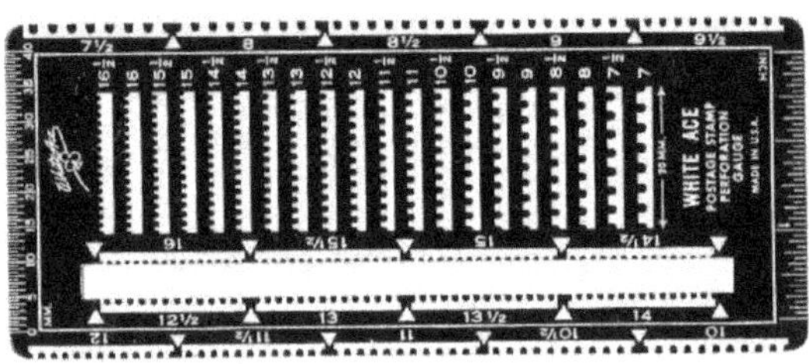

6. **Perforation Gauge:** A perforation gauge measures the number of perforations (or "teeth") on the edges of a stamp. This information is crucial for identifying and cataloguing stamps.

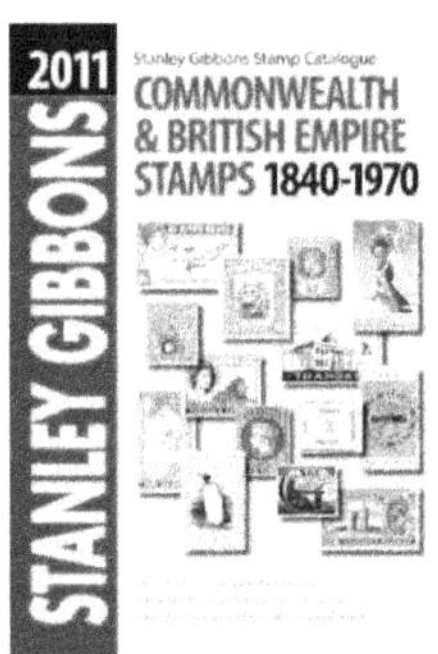

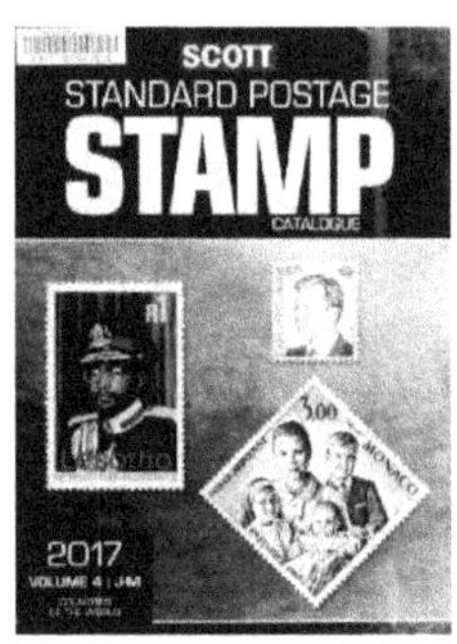

7. **Stamp Catalogue:** A stamp catalogue, such as the Scott Catalogue or the Stanley Gibbons Catalogue provides information about stamps, including their design, history, and current market values.

These are some of the basic accessories stamp collectors use to enhance their hobby and protect their collections. Depending on the size and scope of your collection, you may also invest in additional specialized tools and accessories.

7

Philatelic Material Selection and Exhibition Standards

A Comprehensive Guide

Varieties of Materials Suitable for Philatelic Purposes:

<table>
<tr><td valign="top">

Postal Stationary

- Postal Cards
- Envelopes
- Registered Envelopes
- Letter Sheets/ Inland Letter
- Wrappers
- Aerogramme
- Telegram

Stamps

- Singles
- Pairs
- Multiples - strips or blocks
- Plate Number - strips or blocks
- Coils
- Booklet Panes
- Souvenir Sheets
- Miniature Sheets
- Full Sheets
- Marginal Inscriptions

Stamp Varieties

- Paper
- Perforation
- Watermark
- Gum
- Tagging
- Self - adhesive
- Colour
- Plate

</td><td valign="top">

Stamp Types

- Definitive
- Commemorative
- Airmail
- Official
- Postage Due
- Revenue
- Perfins
- Pre-cancel
- Revalued
- Overprinted
- Surcharged

Cancellations

- Hand
- Machine
- Meter
- Slogan
- Pictorial
- Early Fancy
- Spray-on
- Military - APOs
- Purple/Red Colour
- Socked on the Nose (SOTN)

Covers

- Commercially used (Preferred)
- First Day Cover
- Special Cover
- Airmail
- Domestic/Foreign Destination
- Registered
- Early Usage

</td></tr>
</table>

Other Items	Covers
<ul><li>Errors</li><li>Freaks</li><li>Oddities</li><li>Picture Post Card</li><li>Maximum Card</li><li>Drawings and Sketches on Title</li><li>Proofs</li></ul>	<ul><li>Certified</li><li>Insured</li><li>Special Delivery</li><li>With Other Auxiliary Markings</li><li>Unusual/ Under/ Free Franked</li><li>Souvenir</li><li>First Flight</li></ul>

Materials Not Suitable For Consideration:

1. Stamps depicting fictional postal territories and issues related to exiled governments or organizations lacking postal services are not suitable.

2. Private additional cancellations applied by senders or suppliers prior to mailing the document are discouraged.

3. Picture postcards should be excluded unless they are official postal stationery produced by a Postal Authority or have been commercially used.

4. Private additional prints on postal stationery, also referred to as "Repiquage", should be omitted.

5. Administrative marks that lack postal significance are not to be included.

6. Private decorations on envelopes and cards should be excluded from consideration.

7. Private vignettes, including advertising labels, regardless of their purpose, are not appropriate for inclusion.

8. Genuine commercial mail with relevant cancellations is preferable over mere souvenir documents and similar items designed solely for collector satisfaction. This includes decorated First Day Covers (FDCs), even when issued by the postal service.

8

How to Build a Philatelic Exhibit

An Incremental Walkthrough

Building a philatelic exhibit is a rewarding and creative way to showcase your collection of postage stamps and related materials. Whether you're a beginner or an experienced philatelist, here is a brief guide on how to create an engaging philatelic exhibit:

1. **Choose a Theme:** Start by selecting a specific theme or topic for your exhibit. This theme could be based on a country, a historical event, a particular type of stamp, or any other philatelic interest you have. Your theme should be unique and interesting.

2. **Research and Gather Materials:** Thoroughly research your chosen theme. Gather stamps, covers, postcards, and other philatelic items that relate to your theme. Make sure to acquire these materials through legitimate sources such as stamp dealers, auctions, or exchanges. "List of suitable materials that can be used in building a philatelic exhibit is given in the previous chapter."

3. **Organize Your Collection:** Organize your materials in a logical order. Decide how you want to present your exhibit. Common organizational approaches include chronological, geographical, thematic, or a combination of these. Use archival-quality materials to protect your stamps and covers.

4. **Plan the Layout:** Create a layout plan for your exhibit. Decide how many frames or pages you will use, and allocate space for each item. Ensure the arrangement is visually appealing and tells a coherent story about your chosen theme.

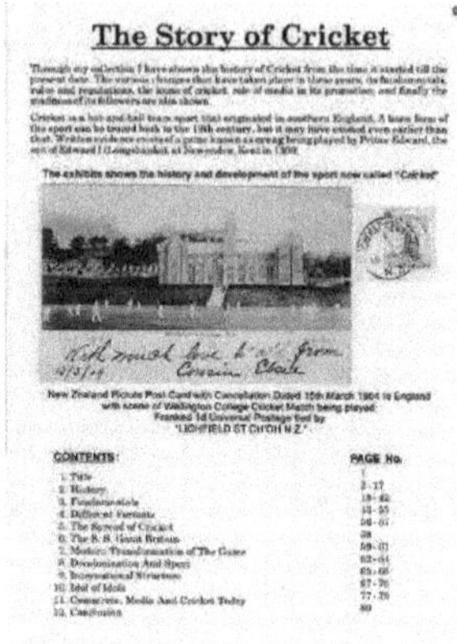

[Unambiguous Exhibit Title]

[Clear Purpose, Scope, and additional information for viewing and understanding the exhibit]

[Appropriate Material to begin the story]

[Exhibit Plan]

5. **Write Descriptive Text:** Each item in your exhibit should be accompanied by descriptive text or captions. Write informative and concise descriptions that provide context, historical background, and interesting facts about the stamps or covers. Use clear and legible fonts.

6. **Include Supporting Material:** Enhance your exhibit with supporting materials such as maps, drawings and sketches used in bringing those particular materials into existence. These can help to illustrate the theme better and make your exhibit more engaging.

7. **Follow Philatelic Rules:** Familiarize yourself with the rules and guidelines of philatelic exhibiting. Fédération Internationale de Philatélie (FIP) is the global governing body for organized philately. It establishes/oversees international standards and rules for philatelic exhibitions, including the criteria for judging exhibits and the guidelines for exhibitors.

Common rules include restrictions on item size, presentation format, and labelling.

8. **Proofread and Edit:** Review your exhibit thoroughly for accuracy, clarity and completeness. Make sure all text is error-free and that the layout flows logically.

9. **Seek Feedback:** Share your exhibit with fellow philatelists or experts to get feedback. They can provide valuable insights and suggestions for improvement.

10. **Assemble and Display:** Once you're satisfied with your exhibit, assemble it in the desired format, whether it's traditional frames, digital displays, or online platforms. Ensure that everything is secure and well-presented.

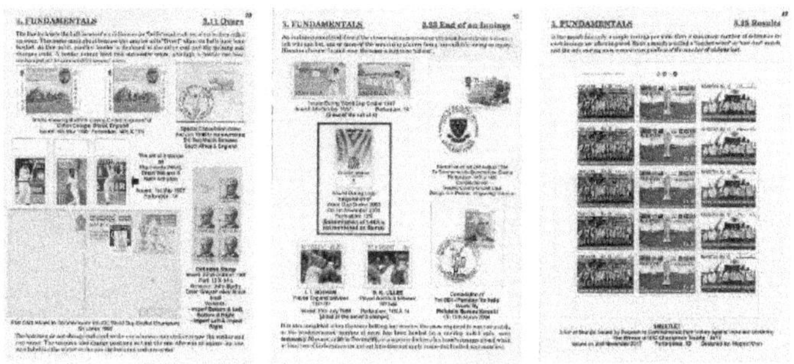

Some Examples of Layout of a Philatelic Exhibit

11. **Enter Exhibitions:** Consider entering your philatelic exhibit into local, regional or national stamp exhibitions. This will allow you to share your collection with a wider audience and receive feedback from judges and other collectors.

12. Maintain and Update: Continuously update and refine your exhibit as you acquire new items or learn more about your chosen theme. Philatelic exhibits are dynamic, and ongoing improvement can lead to greater success in future exhibitions.

Building a philatelic exhibit requires patience, attention to detail, and a passion for stamp collecting. By following these steps and investing time and effort, you can create a compelling and educational display that showcases the beauty and historical significance of your stamp collection.

Additional Guidelines:

1. Mention the page number on the front side of the exhibits.

2. Do not label the material type (e.g., FDC, Special Cover, and Miniature Sheet) above or below the items used.

3. Minimize the use of non-philatelic materials; if necessary, justify their relevance to the theme.

4. Avoid repeating items unless there are significant differences (e.g., perforation variations, color changes, overprints, errors).

5. Use FDCs sparingly to avoid negative marking in exhibitions.

6. Generic cancellations can be used for their specific geographic or thematic significance.

7. Restrict the use of CTO's (Cancel to order).

8. Limit the use of Maximum Cards to enhance the understanding of the subject, focusing on significant items.

9

The Philatelic Dictionary

Exploring The World of Stamps

The Stamp Collectors' Dictionary is a comprehensive reference book that provides collectors with essential information and terminology related to the world of stamp collecting.

(A)

- **Above Privilege Number:** A hand stamp applied to a letter disallowed under the Franking system.

- **Accessories:** Full range of stamp collecting tools and aids, e.g. tweezers, hinge mounts, perforation gauges, catalogues, stock books, catalogues and books etc.

- **Additional Halfpenny Tax:** The Additional Halfpenny Tax was imposed on 8 June 1813 on all letters from England to or from Scotland to recover a levy paid to the Scottish Turnpike Trusts.

- **Add-On:** A cachet design added to a cover which was originally uncacheted.

- **Adhesive:** (i) Any postage stamp for attachment to an envelope, as distinct from the stamps impressed directly onto postal stationery. (ii) The gum used to affix a postage stamp.

- **Admirals:** Philatelic term for three British Commonwealth definitive series stamps: Canada 1912 - 25, New Zealand 1926 and Rhodesia 1913 - 19. All of which show King George V in his naval uniform.

- **Advertisement Pane:** A pane of postage stamps from a booklet in which one or more of the stamp-sized areas bears an advertisement or slogan.

- **Aerogramme:** Printed and gummed writing-sheet designed to be folded and sealed to form a lightweight airmail letter. Usually made of thin paper and printed with the appropriate postal duty. No enclosures are permitted.

- **Aero-Philately:** Area of stamp collecting which concentrates on mail carried by air.

- **Agency:** Post office maintained by one country in another country's territory.

- **Air Label:** Small blue labels used by UPU member nations to denote carriage by airmail.

- **Airmail:** Carriage of mail by aircraft. The first successful mail flight was in May 1911 when Captain Windham organized a flight at the Allahabad Exhibition in India. Special postmarks subsequently came into general use.

- **Airmail Stamp:** A stamp intended for use on mail to be carried by aircraft.

- **Albino:** White or without colour; a postage stamp or overprint in which the absence of ink has resulted in a colourless impression.

- **Album:** Books used for mounting and displaying stamps or postal history. They come in a great variety of colours, sizes and speciality topics.

- **Album Weed:** In general, a forged stamp. It also refers to unusual items resembling postage stamps but were not intended to pay postage, like publicity labels and bogus issues. Album Weeds is the title of a reference book series on forged stamps written by the Rev. R. Brisco Ear.

- **Allen, Ralph:** (b.1694, d.1794) Former postmaster of Bath, England and organizer of the first British provincial cross-posts.

- **All Purpose Cachet:** A cachet with a general purpose design that can be used for a variety of different stamp subjects.

- **Alphabet:** A particularly distinctive set of letters used to print a postage stamp or overprint and which helps a philatelist identify the item precisely.

- **Aniline:** Oily liquid, originally distilled from coal-tar, used as the basis of certain dyes in postage stamps; in particular, a bright-red ink manufactured partly from aniline, which immediately penetrates between the fibres of uncoated paper.

- **A.P.O.:** Army Post Office.

- **Approval Selections or 'Approvals':** Stamps sent "on approval", usually by dealers to collectors. The collector selects the stamps he wishes to purchase and returns the balance to the dealer, enclosing payment for the stamps retained. The purchase of stamps from approval selections has always been one of the most interesting and popular ways of building a collection.

- **Apres le Depart:** Too Late.

- **Arrow:** Small arrow markers appearing in the selvage as a guide for cutting a sheet of stamps into pre-defined blocks.

- **Auction:** A public sale at which various lots of stamps are sold to the highest bidder.

- **Ausstellung:** Exhibition (In German Language).

- **Authentication Mark:** A marking, such as initials, placed on the reverse of a stamp examined and certified to be genuine by an expert. Such markings do not detract from the value of the stamps when they represent the endorsement of recognized authorities.

- **Avion:** Air Mail.

(B)

- **B.A.P.O.:** British Army Post Office.

- **B.F.P.O.:** British Force Post Office.

- **B.I.O.T.:** British Indian Ocean Territories.

- **B.N.A.:** British North America
  (Canada, Newfoundland, Nova Scotia, etc).

- **B.W.I.:** British West Indies.

- **B.T.B.:** Believed to be (Abbreviation used by dealers and auction houses. Believed to Be-as described but cannot be guaranteed by the vendor as such).

- **Back Print:** An 'overprint' applied to the back of a stamp.

- **Back Stamp:** A handstamp applied to the back of a letter, usually indicating the date of transit or receipt at the office of destination.

- **Back-of-The-Book:** Stamps that are normally listed in the back of the catalogue after the regular stamp issues. This might include air mail, special delivery, official, semi-official, postage due, local issues, stamped envelopes, postcards, hunting permit stamps, essays, and revenue stamps.

- **Bahnpost:** Railway.

- **Bantams:** The smaller-sized stamps issued by South Africa during WWII to conserve paper.

- **Btonn:** Paper watermarked with straight parallel lines.

- **Bicoloured:** Two coloured; usually refers to a stamp.

- **Bilingual:** Postage stamp printed in two languages.

- **Bilingual Pair:** Se-tenant postage stamps, each printed in a different language.

- **Bisect:** Half a postage stamp postally used for half its original value.

- **Bishop Mark:** The first handstamp, invented by Henry Bishop. A circle divided horizontally, the top segment showing the month and the lower half the day of posting.

- **Blind Perforation:** A perforation hole not punched out (blunt or missing pin), leaving the paper intact but marked. Generally considered to be a minor variety carrying little premium.

- **Blocks:** Four or more un-separated stamps forming a square or rectangle. A block is understood to consist of four stamps unless some other number is specified, such as "block of six", "block of nine", etc.

- **Blued Paper:** The paper of a stamp which has a pale blue tinge as a result of the manufacturing process.

- **Bogus:** Fraudulent postage stamp that pretended to have been issued but never was. Sometimes, it is either a non-existent issue or a non-existent country.

- **Booklet:** Small convenient book containing pages of mint stamps.

- **Booklet Pane:** A block of stamps, usually six, which originally formed a page in one of the small booklets of stamps sold by the post office.

- **Bourse (pronounced "Boorse"):** An exchange or market where stamps are sold or traded.

- **Boxed:** Handstamp or printed marking in the margin of the postage stamp sheet, surrounded by a rectangular lined 'box' frame.

- **Bureau:** The Department where the postal stamps are produced or issued.

- **Burelage:** A postage stamp security background: a pattern of fine wavy lines, often fugitive, printed on the front or back of some postage stamps.

- **Burele:** Adjective form for burelage, meaning having a fine network of lines. Some stamps of Queensland have a burele band on the back. Also called Moir.

- **Burritt, Elihu:** Philanthropist and campaigner for a drastic reduction in an established set of postage rates in use by many different countries. The main proponent of Ocean Penny Postage.

(C)

- **C.A.:** Crown Agents.

- **Cachet:** A picture, design or description printed or rubber-stamped on an envelope to explain the occasion on which the envelope was mailed, such as the first flight over a new airmail route, the first day of issue of a new stamp, etc.

- **Cancelled-to-Order:** Cancelled without being used for postage - government occasionally cancels their remainder stocks (to prevent using the stamps for postage) and sells them to dealers.

- **Cancellation:** The ink-mark or other defacement (cuts, holes) to a stamp to show that it has been used once and may not be used again. Stamps cancelled with pen lines are said to be pen-cancelled. Stamps that are cancelled in advance by having the name of a town or city printed on them are called Per-cancelled stamps or Pre-cancels.

- **Cantered:** In a perfectly perforated sheet of postage stamps, each stamp has the same size of margin on each side; in describing a valuable stamp, it is desirable to comment on the centring by stating the stamp is 'Perfectly Centred' or 'Centred to the Bottom', 'Centred to Top' etc. 'Centred to the Bottom' means the top margin is larger than the bottom one. The term is not applicable to imperfect stamps.

- **Cantonal Stamp:** Issues of Switzerland's cantons (states) used before the release of national stamps. The cantonal issues of Basel (1845), Geneva (1843-50) and Zurich (1843-50) are among the classics of philately.

- **Cape Tringles:** Common name for the triangular Cape of Good Hope stamps of 1853-64, the first stamps printed in triangular format. The distinctive shape helped illiterate postal clerks distinguish letters originating in the colony from those from other colonies.

- **Catalogue Number:** An identifying number assigned to each individual stamp of every country by the publisher of a postage stamp catalogue.

- **Catalogue Value:** The current value or price assigned to a stamp by the publisher of a postage stamp catalogue.

- **C.A.T:** (Abbrev) Catalogue value (unless there is no possibility of doubt, the publisher should be named).

- **C.C.:** Crown Colony.

- **C.D.S.:** (Abbrev) Circular Date Stamp cancel.

- **C.D.S.:** Circular Date Handstamp, the preferred type of cancellation for most modern postage stamps.

- **Censored Mail:** A cover bearing a handstamp or label indicating that the envelope has been opened and the contents inspected by a censor.

- **Centimetre or Cm:** A unit of measurement in the metric system. 2.54 centimetres equals one inch.

- **Certified Mail:** A service of most postal administrations that provides proof of mailing and delivery without indemnity for loss or damage.

- **Chalk Paper:** Describes postage stamps printed on specially treated paper to receive a good printing impression and to resist the removal of cancellations.

- **Changeling:** A stamp whose colour has been changed - intentionally or unintentionally-by contact with a chemical or exposure to light.

- **Charity Stamp:** (i) An adhesive label not intended for postage use issued to support a charity. (ii) A postage stamp bearing a surcharge which, usually after deductions for overheads, is donated by the postal authority to a charity featured in the design of the stamp.

- **Charge Marks:** Before 1840, black figures (either manuscript or stamped) were used for unpaid letters to be settled by the recipient, and red figures were used for paid letters. In the provinces, hand-stamped figures were occasionally used.

- **Cinderella Stamp:** A stamp-like label that is not a postage stamp. Cinderellas include seals and bogus issues, as well as revenue stamps, local post issues and other similar items.

- **Classic:** A stamp, chiefly one issued before 1870, which, because of wide philatelic acceptance, has gained universal popularity and reputation.

- **Cleaning (stamps):** Soiled or stained stamps are sometimes cleaned with chemicals or by erasing. The cleaning is usually done to improve the appearance of a stamp. A cleaned stamp can also mean one from which a cancellation has been removed, making a used stamp appear unused.

- **Clich:** The individual unit consisting of the design of a single stamp combined with others to make up the complete printing plate. Individual designs on modern one-piece printing plates are referred to as subjects.

- **City Penny Post:** The 1765 act (5 George 3 Cap 25) allowed the setting up of "A Penny Post office" in any city in town in Great Britain, Ireland or North America, as though convenient to be the same as the London Penny Post office.

- **Coated Paper:** Any paper bearing a coating, chalky or otherwise.

- **Coil leader:** Piece of paper in the form of a long tag at the delivery end of a coil; usually printed with the number, denomination and coil price, and sometimes with a date or checker's number.

- **Collateral Material:** Any supportive or explanatory material relating to a given stamp or philatelic topic. The material may be either directly postal in nature (post office news releases, rate schedules, souvenir cards, promotional items) or nonpostal (maps, photos of scenes appearing on stamps).

- **Colour Changeling:** A postage stamp whose original colour has changed.

- **Colour Shift:** Where the design of the stamp has more than one colour, and these are applied at different times in the process of printing, and the positioning of the colours is incorrect in relation to the intended design.

- **Colour Trial:** Postage stamp printed singly or in multiple in a particular shade of ink to judge aesthetic appearance prior to the final decision on the issued colour.

- **Column:** A vertical row of postage stamps.

- **Coil Stamps:** Stamps which are used in long, coiled strips, especially for use in vending or affixing machines. Coiled stamps have straight edges on two opposite sides and are perforated on the other two.

- **Comb Perforation:** The perforation of a stamp formed by the pins of the perforating machine, which are arranged like a comb.

- **Combination:** A cover bearing (i) the handstamps or postage stamps of two different countries (ii) Postage stamps of different denominations, not se-tenant.

- **Commatology:** Specialized collecting of postmarks. This term was invented before World War II to describe postmark collecting. It is rarely used. Usually, collectors refer to postmark collecting or marcophily.

- **Commemorative Stamps:** Stamps issued in remembrance of an event or as a memorial to some person.

- **Compound Perforation:** Perforation of two different measurements on the same stamp.

- **Condition:** Factors that can assist in determining the value of a stamp. Factors include colour, selvage, plate or die variations, unusual cancels, faults, hinging, gum, and markings.

- **Condominium:** A Territory over which there is joint rule by two Powers. An example of this is the Anglo-French New Hebrides Condominium, whose stamps are inscribed in English and French.

- **Control:** Letters and/or figures printed in a postage stamp sheet margin to indicate time of accounting, distribution or other manufacturing data.

Examples are sheet serial numbers on the backs of stamps, dates in sheet margins, and overprints added to prevent the use of stolen stocks.

- **Copyright Block:** Block of four or more United States stamps with the copyright notice marginal marking of the United States Postal Service. The copyright marking was introduced in 1978 and replaced the Mail Early marking.

- **Corner Card:** An imprinted return address, generally in the upper-left corner of an envelope, from a commercial, institutional or private source, similar to a business card or letterhead imprint.

- **Counterfeit:** A fraudulent imitation of a genuine postage stamp.

- **COV:** (Abbrev) Cover.

- **Cover:** (1) An envelope minus the letter it contained, letter-sheet or wrapper when postally used. (2) An envelope that has been sent through the mail.

- **C.R.:** Caledonian Railway.

- **Crash Cover:** A cover that has been salvaged from the crash of an airplane, train, ship or other vehicle. Such covers often carry a postal marking explaining damage or delay in delivery.

- **Crease:** A noticeable weakening of the paper of a stamp or cover caused by its being folded or bent at some point. Creases substantially lower a stamp's value. Creases particularly affect cover values when they extend through the attached stamp or a postal marking. Stamp creases are visible in watermark fluid.

- **C.T.O.:** Cancelled To order.

- **Currency Stamp:** Handstamps used by the British and French Post offices, embodying a stated amount of currency. E.g. "GB/40c".

- **Cut Corner:** An area in the upper right corner of an envelope or card that has been removed from the original piece.

- **Cut Square or Envelope Cut Square:** An embossed or printed envelope, postcard, letter-card or letter-sheet stamp cut following ample margin from the entire piece for the sake of convenience.

- **Cut-to-Shape:** A nonrectangular stamp or postal stationery imprint cut to the shape of the design rather than cut square. Cut-to-shape stamps and stationery generally have a lower value than those cut square. One of the world's most valuable stamps, the unique 1856 British Guiana "Penny Magenta", is a cut-to-shape stamp.

- **Cylinder:** The cylinder used to print photogravure postage stamps. In many cases, the cylinder is numbered and is large enough to print two PO sheets of stamps simultaneously. One of the sheets is often called the 'dot sheet' and the other the 'no dot sheet'; thus, the seventh cylinder made for a particular issue would print sheets bearing the numbers 7 and 7, the latter being read as 'seven dots'.

- **Cylinder Block:** Block of postage stamps (usually six) from that part of the sheet where the cylinder number(s) can be seen in the margin.

- **Cylinder Number:** The number(s) printed in the margin of a postage stamp sheet by each cylinder used to print the sheet; thus, a seven-colour stamp will have seven cylinder numbers, each in the colour of one of the chosen inks, with an additional number for any cylinder used to print phosphor tagging.

(D)

- **Dandy Roll:** The wire mesh roller used in papermaking to produce a watermark.

- **Date Stamp:** A hand or machine stamp containing a date; sometimes used to mean C.D.S.

- **Dead Country:** A former stamp-issuing entity that has ceased issuing its own stamps. Also, the old name of an active stamp-issuing entity that has changed its name, so that the old name will no longer be usedon stamps.

- **Definitive:** A postage stamp intended to remain in everyday use for a considerable time as distinct from a provisional, commemorative or other special issue.

- **Deltiology:** Picture postcard collecting.

- **Denomination:** The monetary and postal value of a stamp as "Rs.5", "1 cent", "2 shillings", etc.

- **Des.:** Abbreviation for 'designed by'.

- **Die:** The original single engraved piece of metal from which a multiple-printing plate is built.

- **Die Proof:** Single, very carefully impressed proof of a new postage stamp die, invariably in black ink on smooth white card or fine-calendared or coated paper. When dry, inspect in great detail to check that the die is perfect.

- **Directory Markings:** Postal indication of failed delivery attempt, stating the reason for failure. Examples are "No Such Number", "Address Unknown", and "Moved".

- **Disaster Mail:** Mail carried on ships or aircraft that were damaged. It has been the custom of the Post office to put special marks on the recovered mail to explain the damage.

- **Doctor Blade:** A steel blade which wipes ink from the cylinder.

- **Dot, No Dot:** The cylinder used to print photogravure postage stamps. In many cases, the cylinder is numbered and is large enough to print two PO sheets of stamps simultaneously. One of the sheets is often called the 'dot sheet' and the other the 'no dot sheet'; thus, the seventh cylinder made for a particular issue would print sheets bearing the numbers 7 and 7, the latter being read as 'seven dots'.

- **Double-Ring C.D.S.:** A circular date handstamp contained within two concentric circles.

- **Doubly Printed:** Postage stamp or part of sheet bearing more than one clear impression of the printed design, invariably both on the same side of the sheet and both in the same sense (i.e. not an offset).

- **Dry Print:** Postage stamp image or overprint grossly deficient in ink, but not albino (which is devoid of any ink).

- **Duck Stamps:** Popular name for the United States Migratory Bird Hunting and Conservation stamp, issued for use on hunting licenses. Each annual stamp depicts waterfowl. It is also used to describe similar issues from the various states for use by hunters or sale to collectors.

- **Due:** Adhesive label to record postage due on delivery because of insufficient prepayment.

- **Dulwich Mark:** First trailed in 1894, the Dulwich type of double arc dated postmark became the standard British type for many years.

- **Dumb Cancellation:** An obliteration handstamp containing neither figure nor letter, often made of cork. Used for a variety of purposes, including cancellation of postage stamps, Wartime security cancelling, and postage census.

- **Dummy Stamps:** Officially produced imitation stamps used to train employees or to test automatic stamp-dispensing machines. Dummy stamps are usually blank or carry special inscriptions, blocks or other distinguishing ornamentation. They are not valid for postage, nor are they intended to reach the hands of stamp collectors. Some do in favour of postal employees.

- **Duplex:** A cancellation handstamp embodying two sections, one to obliterate the adhesive and a second portion to indicate the office and date of posting. Strictly speaking, most Double Date stamps are not true Duplexes. True Duplex stamps have the two elements combined in one design, such as the spoon and shoe type.

- **Duplicate:** An additional copy of a stamp that one already has in a collection. Beginners often consider stamps to be duplicates that really are not because they overlook perforation, watermark or colour varieties.

- **Duty Plate:** Portion of a postage stamp design containing the postal duty (face value) when printed separately from the frame, head, or key plate; in particular, the plate used to impress the duty.

(E)

- **E.A.F.:** East African Forces.

- **E.L.:** Entire Letter.

- **Einschreiben:** Registered.

- **E.K.U.:** The cover or piece that documents the earliest date on which a stamp or postal. stationery item is known to be used. New discoveries can change an established E.K.U. The E.K.U. for a classic issue may be after the official issue date. Because of accidental early sales, the E.K.U. for modern stamps is often several days before the official first day.

- **Embossing:** The process by which part of the design of a stamp is 'raised'.

- **Encased Postage Stamp:** A stamp inserted into a small coin-size case with a transparent front or back. Such stamps were circulated as legal coins during periods when coins were scarce.

- **End Delivery:** Coil in which postage stamps are arranged 'one above the other' and dispensed by a machine.

- **Engraving:** The process of producing a stamp design from a metal or wood plate.

- **Engraved:** A method of printing in which the lines of the design are cut into metal, which are recessed to retain the ink. The paper is forced under pressure into these lines to pick up the ink. Therefore, the engraved cachets appear to have a design raised above the surface of the paper.

- **Entire:** A stamped envelope, wrapper, postal card or other postal stationary in its entire state, as sold by post offices.

- **Envelope Stamp:** A stamp printed directly on an envelope as distinguished from the separately printed or "adhesive" stamp.

- **Errors:** Stamps with wrong design, colour, printing, paper, perforation or overprinting, unintentionally issued by the post office.

- **Essay:** A stamp produced for trial or experimental purposes prior to the issue of the final agreed design.

- **Est.:** Estimated Price, which an auctioneer thinks would be a fair price for a particular lot.

- **Etiquette:** An adhesive which is not a postage stamp.

- **Event Cover:** A cached cover prepared as a souvenir of a specific event or an anniversary of an event.

- **Expertization:** The examination of a stamp or cover by an acknowledged expert to determine if it is genuine. As standard procedure, an expert or expertizing body issues a signed certificate, often with an attached photograph, attesting to theitem's status.

- **Exploded:** A stamp booklet that has been separated into its various components, usually for display purposes. Panes are removed intact: individual stamps are not separated from the pane.

- **Express Mail:** Next-day mail delivery service in the United States, inaugurated in 1977.

- **Extension Perf Hole:** Pattern of perforation in which each horizontal (rarely, each vertical) row of perforations is extended by one hole into either or both margins.

(F)

- **Face Value:** The value as indicated by the figures, words or abbreviations in the design or the surcharge of the stamp.

- **Facsimile:** Printed copy of a (usually rare) postage stamp, with no intent to mislead.

- **Fake:** An originally genuine stamp which has been illegitimately altered by adding or removing perforations, chemically changing the colour, applying a surcharge, overprint or cancellation, etc. to increase its philatelic value.

- **Fancy Cancel:** A cancellation which is or includes a design.

- **Fast Colors:** Inks resistant to fading.

- **Faults:** Factors that can decrease the value of a stamp. E.g. thin spots, creases, short or torn perforations, missing pieces, tears or stains.

- **F.B.O.:** Foreign Branch Office.

- **Field Post office (F.P.O.):** A post office for military forces on active service.

- **Fifth Clause Post:** Handstamps so inscribed (relative to the 5th Clause of an Act of Parliament concerning village posts).

- **File Crease:** Cover or other postal items that have been kept folded over a long period.

- **Filler:** A stiff piece of paper or cardboard found inside a First Day Cover. It provides the necessary stiffness for a clearer cancellation. It also provides protection to help prevent the bending of the cover as it travels through the mail.

- **Fine:** Philatelically sound and desirable, particularly an item in undamaged condition.

- **First Day Cover (F.D.C.):** An envelope bearing a cancellation date representing the first day of issue of the stamp thereon and which is usually mailed from the place where the stamp was first put into circulation.

- **Fiscal:** A stamp issued for revenue or tax purposes and not as a postage stamp.

- **Flaw:** Visible change in the printed design of a postage stamp due to damage to the printing surface of the plate or cylinder; constant flaws are seen, either unchanged or very slowly progressing, over a large number of stamps printed by the same impression.

- **Fleuron:** A circular date handstamp with two flowers or petal-shaped ornaments at the foot.

- **Forerunner:** A handstamp used by a parent country within an area which subsequently became independent of the original domination.

- **Forgery:** Postal item fraudulently manufactured with intent to deceive either the post office (postal forgery) or collectors (fake).

- **Forwarding Agent's Cachet:** A strike or endorsement applied to a letter to indicate that it had been handled in transit by some means other than the Post office.

- **Frama:** A general name used for an automatic stamp, derived from the name of the Swiss firm, Frama AG, an early producer of such issues. Automatic stamps are produced individually by a machine on demand in a denomination selected by the customer. There normally is no date on the stamp, as there is on a meter stamp. It is also called A.T.M., from the German word Automatenmarken.

- **Frame:** Printed border of a postage stamp.

- **Frank:** A stamp, mark or signature that shows payment of postage on a piece of mail.

- **Franking:** Any devices, markings or combinations thereof ("franks") applied to mails of any class which qualifies them to be postally serviced.

- **Free Frank:** A handstamp applied under the Franking system (until 1840, free postage was enjoyed by Members of Parliament) indicates that the item is to be carried free of charge.

- **Freak:** A stamp showing a production flaw that is not a consistent error, such as one perforated through the middle with an ink smudge, etc.

- **Fresh:** Postal item, especially an adhesive, in fine original colour.

- **F.U.:** Fine Used.

- **Fugitive Lines:** These are inks which are specially produced so that they will change or wash out if there is an attempt to tamper with the stamp, such as, removing the postmark. This is meant to prevent the reuse of stamps already passed through the Postal System.

(G)

- **Gauge:** Number of perforation holes in a length of 20mm (in the case of most definitive, the number of teeth counted across from left to right).

- **G.B.P.:** Great Britain Pound.

- **Gepruft:** Censored (German).

- **G.N.A or Gone no Address:** Undelivered or Returned Mail.

- **Grade:** The ranking of a stamp based on centering for mint stamps, centering and cancellation for used stamps.

- **Granite Paper:** Paper containing countless very short hairs (fibres) of colour(s) contrasting with the main mat of the paper as a security against forgery.

- **Graphite Lines:** A method of marking stamps for automatic mail sorting. Used on some British stamps.

- **Gravure:** A form of recess printing using photo-etching.

- **Grill:** A network of embossed or raised impressions made in a stamp by a metal roll with points. The grill is said to be "points up", if the points show on the face of the stamp and "points down" if on the opposite.

- **Guide Dot/Line:** Dot or line appearing on a postage stamp due to failure to erase punched or inscribed marks on the plate intended to guide the plate-maker in entering the stamp impressions. Usually, such marks are close to the frame of the stamp.

- **Gum:** The adhesive coating on the backs of most unused postage stamps.

- **Gum Arabic:** Widely used adhesive applied as a glossy coating that is transparent when pure but yellowish when less highly refined, obtained from the acacia tree and called gum acacia.

- **Gum Crease:** A crease ironed out of the paper of an unused postage stamp but clearly visible in the gum; in some cases, the crease is actually caused by warping and subsequent of the gum.

- **G.U.:** Good Used.

- **Gutter:** The margin that divides a sheet of stamps.

(H)

- **Hand Cancel:** A cancel that is applied to stamps individually and by hand.

- **Hand Coloured:** A printed, handmade cachet to which hand painting or hand colouring has been added. Also termed as Hand Printed.

- **Hand Drawn:** A cachet applied to a cover by hand with pen, pencil, brush, chalk or other art media.

- **Handmade:** A cachet applied to a cover by hand by adding seals, paste-ups, collages or similar materials. Each cachet is made individually and is an original.

- **Hair line:** Any fine line in a printed postage stamp design, either a printed coloured line on unprinted paper or an unprinted white line on the printed design, in particular, unprinted diagonal lines across the corners of certain British typographed postage stamps of 1862-64.

- **Hand-Stamped:** Stamped or cancelled by hand, usually with a rubber stamp.

- **Harrow Perforation:** A means of perforating a whole sheet at a time.

- **Head Plate:** In a postage stamp printed by two or more impressions, usually in contrasting colours, the portion of the design containing the central portion (which in early stamps generally contained a portrait).

- **Heaton, Henniker:** Conservation Member of Parliament for Canterbury and champion of the idea of a Universal Penny Postage introduced in June 1898.

- **Heavy Cancel:** Destruction which, either by its design or over-inking, spoils the appearance of the adhesive stamp by covering most of its surface.

- **High Value:** The term applied to stamps which represent a higher value of postage. Not to be confused with the actual market value of a stamp.

- **Hill, Pearson:** Popularly known as the father of the cancelling machine. In 1857, he produced a machine which could be operated by steam or a foot treadle to apply a duplex stamp automatically.

- **Hill, Rowland:** Organiser of uniform postage in Britain. His 4d uniform postage reform and subsequently, 1d uniform postage reform led to the introduction of the world's first postage stamp, The Penny black.

- **Hinges:** Small rectangles of thin semi-transparent paper, gummed on one side, used for mounting or affixing stamps to album pages.

- **Historical Covers:** Envelopes that are cancelled with reference to a historical event. E.g., the coronation of a King, President, etc. Also termed as Inaugural Cover.

- **H.P.O.:** Highway Post office. Portable mail-handling equipment for sorting mail in transit on highways (normally by truck). The last official U.S. HPO ran June on 30, 1974.

- **Hutchins, Thomas:** Postmaster at Crewkerne, he built up an early form of Postal Trade union. In 1630, he obtained the first authorisation to carry private letters. This, of course, was a major event. For the first time, authority had been given to carriage private mail within the State Postal System. Thus was laid the foundation of the first public horse post.

(I)

- **I.B.:** Inland Branch.

- **Imperforate:** Without perforation; having straight edges on all sides.

- **Impression:** The image of a postage stamp transferred by pressure to a duplicate die or transfer roller.

- **Imprimatur:** In philately, usually a postage stamp cut from one of the first sheets to be printed of a new design or new plate, often on un-gummed paper and usually imperf, frequently the issued stamps were perforated and of a different shade of ink.

- **Imprint:** The imprint of the designer or producer of the stamp which is printed on the stamp.

- **India Letter:** A ship letter handstamp applied to letters arriving from central of Africa and India.

- **Indicium:** The stamp impression of a postage meter or the imprint on postal stationery (as opposed to an adhesive stamp), indicating prepayment and postal validity. Plural: indicia.

- **Inscription:** The letter, words or character appearing on a stamp as an integral part of the overall design.

- **Intaglio:** Line-engraved or recess printing, as used for the 'Penny Black'.

- **International Reply Coupon (I.R.C):** A redeemable certificate issued by member nations of the Universal Postal Union to provide for return postage from recipients in other countries. IRCs are exchangeable for postage at a post office.

- **Inv:** Abbreviation for inverted, usually referring to the watermark.

- **Invert:** A stamp with one part (usually the central design) upside down in relation to another part.

- **I.S.:** Inland Section.

- **Item:** General term used for any philatelic materials such as postage stamp, FDC, Booklet, die proof, etc.

- **Ivory Head:** Where the Queen's Head on Queen Victoria stamps show white on the back of blued stamps.

(J)

- **Joint Issue:** Two or more stamps issued by different countries to commemorate the same event, topic, place or person.

- **Jubilee line:** Coloured line framing stamps in the sheet margin.

(K)

- **Key type:** A basic stamp design utilized for the issues of two or more postal entities, usually differing in the country name and inscription of value. Many of the earlier colonial issues of Britain, France, Spain, Germany and Portugal are key types.

- **Kiloware:** A stamp mixture of miscellaneous postally used stamps on envelope corner paper from various sources, sold in kilogramme bags at a flat rate.

(L)

- **Label:** Any small adhesive, other than a valid postage stamp, affixed to a postal item.

- **Ladies' Envelope:** Embossed envelopes used by feminine letter-writers of the 19th Century.

- **Laid Paper:** Paper watermarked with close parallel lines, much wider spaced, crossing at right angles.

- **Last Day:** The final day of a postal rate, post office operation or similar occurrence.

- **Late Fee:** The fee charged on a letter which had been posted subsequent to normal 'last collection' time, additional to the ordinary postage.

- **Letterpress:** Typography or surface printing from relief plates.

- **Letter Sheet:** A sheet of writing paper with a stamp printed on it so that the sheet can be folded, sealed, addressed and mailed with an outside appearance somewhat resembling a stamped envelope.

- **Lift to:** To unstick an adhesive from a cover or any other substrate.

- **Line engraving:** The process of making a stamp design on metal plates using a series of lines to form the design in steel or copper plate. Pioneered by Perkins & Bacon, Printers. The image is cut into a steel or copper plate to create a 'Master' die in reverse, then the plate is hardened, which is then impressed onto a softer metal plate or roller. The roller is then hardened, and the design is again transferred onto a thin plate that will form the printing plate.

- **Lithography:** The process of printing from a flat plate.

- **Line Pair:** A line of ink printed between two coil stamps at various intervals.

- **Line Perf:** Abbreviated description for a stamp or sheet perforated in straight lines, all the horizontal (or vertical) lines being done first and then all the crossing lines. The two sets of perforations need not register at the corners of the stamps.

- **Lightly Hinged:** A stamp with full gum with only slight evidence of hinge marks or disturbance.

- **Litho:** Lithography.

- **Lithography:** A process for printing in which the inked image is determined by the ability of a flat surface to repel ink in some places and hold it in others (where it is greasy).

- **L.M.M.:** Lightly Mounted Mint.

- **Local Stamp:** A stamp whose use is limited to a particular area within a country.

- **L.P.S.:** London Postal Section.

- **Luftpost:** Airmail (German).

- **Luminescent:** The condition of a stamp which has been treated with chemicals which are sensitive to and glow under ultraviolet light.

(M)

- **M:** Mint.

- **Machin:** A definitive stamp of Great Britain which is in current use. Designed by Amold Machin.

- **Major Varieties:** Stamps differing in one or more major respects, such as design, denomination, colour, shape, size, paper, perforation, watermark, imprints, inscriptions, etc., either in the same or different dates of issue.

- **Make-Up:** The contents of a stamp booklet, usually in total number of stamps of each denomination.

- **Marcophily:** Postmark collecting.

- **Margin:** The unprinted paper surrounding the design on a stamp.

- **Marginal Rule:** Printed line, usually about 0.1 in (2.5 mm) wide, surrounding the stamp impressions on a sheet. Usually, one line is used for each ink used to print the stamps, and the rule is often broken at the gutters. It is impressed by a raised edge around the printing plate, which reduces or eliminates the shock that would otherwise be felt as the inking roller stricks the first row of stamp images on the plate.

- **Marque D'entrée:** (French) The handstamp applied to a letter indicative of its having entered another country.

- **Mat:** A hard rubber plate used to apply overprints on postage stamps.

- **Maximaphily:** Maximum card collecting.

- **Maximum Card:** Envelope or postcard bearing a printed, usually illustrated, feature linked with the subject, if commemorative stamp with which it is postally used (not necessarily on the day of issue).

- **MC:** "Maltese Cross" cancel. Used to cancel Queen Victoria stamps, e.g. 1d Black. These may be in black, red, yellow, blue or magenta and comprise an eight-pointed cross.

- **Meter:** The mechanical or digital device that creates a valid denominated postage imprint known as a meter stamp. Postage is prepaid to the regulating postal authority. Meters were authorized by the UPU in 1920. They are used today by volume mailers to cut the cost of franking mail.

- **Mileage Stamp:** A town handstamp embodying a number showing the mileage from London, Edinburgh or Dublin.

- **Military Stamps:** Issued usually in time of war, for use by a country's army and military personnel.

- **Miniature Sheet (MS):** A smaller than regular size sheet, consisting of 1 to 25 stamps - specially printed by a government for a specific event or purpose. The stamps can be either perforated or imperforated, and the sheet with or without inscription.

- **Minor Varieties:** Seemingly similar stamps which differ in some minor respect such as shade of colour or paper; imperfections in design, printing or perforations; positioning of watermark, etc.

- **Mint or Mint Condition:** A stamp which is in the same physical condition as when it left the printing source of supply with full, original gum, never hinged, cancelled, soiled, stained, creased or torn.

- **Mirror Image:** An offset negative or reverse impression.

- **Missent:** A letter misspent (usually through an illegible address) to the wrong town and applied to indicate the reason for the delay in delivery.

- **Mixed Franking:** A cover franked with adhesives of two different issues of adhesives (but usually applied to two different reigns or two different currencies).

- **Mixed Perforation:** Compound Perforation. Different gauge perforations on different sides of a single stamp. The sides with the different gauge measurements are usually perpendicular.

- **Mixture:** A miscellaneous lot of unsorted stamps, usually containing many duplicates and with the stamps frequently on bits of paper, just as torn from envelopes and wrappers.

- **MNH:** Mint Never Hinged.

- **Mobile Post office (MPO):** Portable mail-handling equipment and personnel, generally in railroad cars, streetcars, trucks or buses.

- **Mount(s):** 1. Stamp hinges, 2. Affixing or mounting of stamps on album pages, sheets, etc. 3. Transparent, acetate protective pockets in several sizes for enclosing both single stamps and blocks of four.

- **Moveable Box:** A box in which letters could be posted on board the ship. The box was handed, locked and with its contents, to the post office at which the vessel arrived.

- **M/S.:** Manuscript, i.e. written by hand.

- **Mulready:** A printed letter sheet or envelope issued in 1840 having a pictorial design. William Mulready was the designer of these letter sheets and envelopes.

- **Multiple:** Three or more unseparated stamps, mint or used, on cover or off, in any arrangement.

- **Mute Cancellation:** An obliteration handstamp containing neither figure nor letter, often made of cork. Used for various purposes, including cancellation of postage stamps, Wartime security cancelling, and postage census.

(N)

- **N:** Normal (Price).

- **New Issue:** The latest stamp or series of stamps issued by a country. A "Recent Issue" refers to stamps issued within a few years prior to a "New Issue".

- **New Issue Service:** A dealer service that automatically supplies subscribers with new issues of a given country, area or topic. The issues provided are determined by a prearranged standing order that defines the quantity and types of issues.

- **Newspaper Stamps:** Postage stamps issued for postage on newspapers.

- **N. F.:** Overprint on Nyasaland Stamps was intended to be N.F.F. for Nyasaland Field Force.

- **N/H:** Never Hinged. A stamp without hinge marks. A never-hinged (N/H) stamp usually has original gum, but this is not always the case.

- **N.P.B.:** News Paper Branch.

- **Non-Denominated:** A stamp with no numerical inscription designating the face value. The value of some non-denominated stamps is marked by a designated letter. Others may have a service inscription that indicates the rate of the stamp.

(O)

- **O:** Ordinary.

- **Obliterator:** Hand or machine stamp used to cancel an adhesive, especially a device other than a cds.

- **Obsolete:** No longer in use - a term applied to stamps that are no longer being issued or distributed by post offices.

- **Occupation Stamp:** Stamps issued by one country for use in conquered or occupied territory of another nation.

- **Offices Abroad:** At various times, many nations have maintained post offices in other countries, usually because of the unreliability of the local postal system. In China and the Turkish Empire, especially, many foreign nations maintained their own postal systems as part of their extraterritorial powers. Usually, special stationery and stamps were used by these offices. Most consisted of overprints on the regular issues of the nation's maintaining the offices.

- **Official Stamp:** Stamps which are issued for use by government departments. E.g. Tax, Military.

- **Offset Printing:** A method of printing which consists of transferring or "offsetting" the design from the printing plates to a rubber roller and from the roller to the paper.

- **Offset Lithography:** Surface printing from a cylinder.

- **O.G.:** Original Gum, i.e. bearing most of its original gum in undisturbed condition (but hinged at least once).

- **OHMS:** Abbreviation for on His (or Her) Majesty's Service. Used in perfins, overprints or franks to indicate official use in the British Commonwealth.

- **Omnibus Issues:** Stamps issued with a common design across many countries.

- **On Cover:** A stamp still affixed to the piece of mail on which it was originally issued.

- **On, off Paper:** On paper means a piece had been torn from a postal item containing one or more stamps (but not necessarily including any complete postmarks); off paper means a stamp has been lifted.

- **Ordinary:** Ordinary paper, as distinct from chalky or some other distinctive paper.

- **O.P.:** Overprint. Also written as "Ovpt".

- **Original Gum or O. G.:** The unimpaired gum with which the stamp was originally issued.

- **Overprint:** Any additional printing (surcharging, hand-stamping, overprinting, etc.) on a stamp after the stamp itself has been printed.

- **Oxidation:** Darkening of the ink on certain stamps caused by contact with air or light. Some inks used to print stamps, especially oranges, may turn brown or black in time.

(P)

- **P:** Proof.

- **Packet:** Early term for a fast mailboat operating, as far as wind and weather allowed, to a stated schedule between ports; Small envelope, with transparent front, filled with dealer's common stamps.

- **Pair:** Two un-separated stamps; a "vertical pair" when one stamp is above the other; a "horizontal pair" when side by side.

- **Palmer, John:** Established the first British mail coach service in 1784 and supervised the subsequent growth of the mail coach service until his retirement in 1792.

- **Pane:** The so-called "sheets" of stamps sold by post offices, more correctly termed panes. Most stamps are actually printed in much larger-sized sheets and then divided into smaller, equal-sized units or panes for distribution to post offices.

- **Paper Fault:** Clearly visible irregularity in paper introduced at the time of manufacture of the paper or at least prior to stamp printing.

- **Parcel Post Stamps:** Special stamps created for payment of parcel post fees.

- **Part Perforation:** A stamp with all perforations missing on one or more sides but with at least one side perforated.

- **Paste-Up:** The ends of rolls of coiled stamps joined together with glue or tape.

- **Paquebot: An** international term used to cancel stamps on mail posted on board merchant ships or cancelled at a port foreign to the country whose stamp it bears.

- **P.C.:** Post Cards.

- **P.D.:** Paid To Destination.

- **Peel and Stick:** Australian terminology for 'Self Adhesive'.

- **Pelure:** A type of paper calendared under extreme pressure and thus very thin and often brittle.

- **Pen Cancelled:** Adhesive stamp used postally and cancelled by hand-writing across it.

- **Penny Post:** A local post; one penny is charged for letters delivered within its surroundings.

- **PercEen Arc:** Rouletted by lines of small cured arcs.

- **Perceen Scie:** Rouletted by lines of zig-zag cuts.

- **Perfin:** Normal stamps with initials formed in the stamp by perforations. Often used by commercial organisations as a security measure.

- **Perforation Gauge:** A gauge or scale for determining the perforation number or number of perforation holes in a space of 2 centimetres along the edge of a stamp.

- **Permit:** Franking by the imprint of a number and additional information that identifies a mailer's prepaid postage account, thereby eliminating the need to affix and cancel stamps on large mailings. The mailer must obtain a document (permit) that authorizes his use of this procedure.

- **Phantom Philately:** The collection of bogus stamps. The name is derived from Frederick Melville's book Phantom Philately, one of the pioneer works on bogus issues.

- **Philatelist:** A person who has the hobby of philately or collecting stamps.

- **Philately:** The technical name for postal stamp collecting.

- **Phosphor Stamps:** Stamps which have been coated with a 'fluorescent' substance for detection in the mail sorting system.

- **Phosphor Bands:** A narrow line of 'fluorescent' substance across the face of a stamp. Stamps can have one or two bands, and the position may vary.

- **Photogravure:** Printing process whereby a copper plate is coated with a light-sensitive gelatin tissue which had been exposed to a film positive and then etched, resulting in a high-quality print that can reproduce the details of the stamp.

- **Pictorials:** Stamps bearing pictures, as distinguished from those with portraits, symbolic designs, etc.

- **Pin Hole:** A small hole in a stamp other than perforation applied officially and thus taken as damaged.

- **Pigeon Post:** Use of homing pigeons to carry messages.

- **Plate:** The basic printing unit on a press used to produce stamps. Early stamps were printed from flat plates. Curved or cylindrical plates are used for most modern stamps.

- **Plate Block:** A block of stamps from the corner or side of a pane, including the selvage bearing the number(s) of the plate(s) used to print the sheet from which the pane was separated. Some stamp production methods, like booklet production, usually cut off plate numbers. In the United States, plate number blocks are normally collected as blocks of four to 20 stamps, depending on the press used to print the stamps. When each stamp in a pane is a different design, the entire pane is collected as the plate block.

- **Plate Number:** A file or index number engraved in a plate from which stamps are printed. This number, which is used to help in filing and keeping track of the plates, is usually found in the corner margin of the sheet.

- **Plating:** The reconstruction of a stamp pane by collecting blocks and individual stamps representing various positions. This is possible for many older issues, but most modern issues are too uniform to make the identification of individual positions possible.

- **Pneumatic Post:** Letter distribution through pressurized air tubes. Pneumatic posts existed in many large European cities, and special stamps and stationery were often produced for the service.

- **P.O.A.:** Post Office Agency or Price on Application.

- **Polyvinyl Alcohol:** The preferred gum of many modern postal administrations.

- **Positional Piece:** Portion of a sheet of postage stamp, usually containing a variety, extending to the corner of the sheet or the part of the margin containing marks sufficient to identify the exact location of the variety and thus confirming that the variety is genuine.

- **Postage Due:** A stamp which is used by the postal authorities to indicate that the correct postal fee has not been paid and the sum due for the delivery of the item. Same as 'To Pay' labels.

- **Postal History:** The study of postal markings, rates and routes, or anything to do with the history of the posts.

- **Postal Stationary:** Stationery bearing imprinted stamps, as opposed to adhesive stamps. Postal stationery includes postal cards, letter cards, stamped envelopes, wrappers, aerograms, telegraph cards, postal savings forms and similar government-produced items. The cost to the mailer is often the price of postage plus an additional charge for the stationery item.

- **Postally Used:** A stamp or cover that has seen legitimate postal use, as opposed to one that has been cancelled-to-order or favor-cancelled. The term "postally used" suggests that an item exists because it was used to carry a personal or business communication without the sender thinking of creating an item to be collected.

- **Poster Stamp:** An advertising label, a little larger than most postage stamps, that originated in the mid-19th century and quickly became a collecting craze, growing in popularity up until World War One and then declining by World War Two until they are now almost forgotten except by collectors of Cinderella stamps.

- **Postmark:** A cancellation which usually gives the place, date and time of cancelling.

- **Posted at Sea:** Any maritime handstamp applied to indicate that the letter had been posted on board ship.

- **P.P.:** Pulled Perforation.

- **Pre Cancel:** A postmark which cancels the stamp prior to use in situations where there is bulk mail, such as in commercial mail.

- **Pres:** Presentation Pack.

- **Press Sheet:** A complete unit of stamps as printed. Stamps are usually printed in large sheets and are separated into two or more panes before shipment to post offices.

- **Printed on Gum:** Printed in error on the reverse side of the sheet (if such a stamp becomes wet, the printed design will become detached).

- **Printer's Waste:** Misprinted, mis-perforated or mis-gummed stamps often created during the normal process of stamp production. Printer's waste is supposed to be destroyed, but such material enters the philatelic market through carelessness and theft.

- **Proof: A** piece of fine card or other high-quality substance on which an impression has been carefully taken from a new die or other printing hardware to check that the design is correct in all respects.

- **Provincial Penny Post:** A local post; one penny is charged for letters delivered within its surroundings.

- **Provisional:** A postage stamp issued for temporary use to meet postal demands until a new or regular stock of stamps can be obtained. The issuance of provisional stamps might be occasioned by a change in name or government, by the occupation of foreign territory, by a change in postal rates, a change of currency, or by the need to provide stamps that are in short supplies.

- **P/SET:** Part Set contains some stamps from an issue.

- **P.T.S.A.:** Priced to Sell at. a term used in auctions where stamps in a lot have been previously priced for retail or approval purposes.

(Q)

- **Quadri Partition:** A block or strip of four stamps that together complete a single design.

- **Quadrille Paper:** Patterned or watermarked paper with criss-cross lines.

- **Quartz lamp:** One of several kinds of electric lamp giving radiation mainly in the ultra-violet part of the spectrum, used for observing phosphors.

(R)

- **R:** Abbreviation for Reprint.

- **Railway Post Office (R.P.O.):** Portable mail-handling equipment for sorting mail in transit on trains. RPOs were used in many countries.

- **R, R.R., R.R.R.:** Degree of rarity (in ascending order).

- **Receiver's Stamp:** A handstamp indicating the name or initials of a receiver of Town or City local letters. 17th and 18th Centuries.

- **Recess Printing:** Line engraved or intaglio printing. Recesses are formed on the plate.

- **Recommande:** Registered.

- **Reconstruction:** Postage stamps whose individual position in a sheet is known (e.g. from corner letters), a complete sheet assembled from (usually) used copies.

- **Redrawn:** A stamp design that has been slightly altered yet maintains the basic design as originally issued.

- **Re-Engrave:** To remark the plate or plates from which a stamp (or issue of stamps) is printed without materially changing the design.

- **Re-Entry:** Where the design of a stamp bears additional printing marks as a result of being passed through the printing process again.

- **Regional:** A postage stamp issued for use in only part of the territory under the authority of the postal administration.

- **Registered Mail:** First-class mail with a numbered receipt, including a valuation of the registered item, for full or limited compensation if the mail is lost. Some countries have issued registered mail stamps. Registered mail is signed for by each postal employee who handles it.

- **Registration Labels:** Adhesive labels indicating the registry number and, often, the city of origin for registered articles sent through the mail.

- **Regular Issue:** Stamps issued for ordinary postage use as distinguished from special purpose stamps for airmail, special delivery, postage due, etc.

- **Regummed:** A postal stamp bearing adhesive from an unauthorised source.

- **Reissue:** An official reprinting of a stamp from an obsolete or discontinued issue. Reissues are valid for postage.

- **Repaired:** Stamps that are damaged (by thin spots, creasing, tearing, etc.) are sometimes very cleverly repaired, but they are still considered damaged, and collectors do not want them.

- **Replica:** A reproduction of a stamp or cover. In the 19th century, replica stamps were sold as stamp album space fillers. Replica stamps are often printed in one colour on a sheet containing a number of different designs. Replicas can sometimes deceive either a postal clerk or a collectors.

- **Reprint:** A stamp printed from the original plates (usually after an issue has become obsolete) but not intended to be used for postage.

- **Retouch:** A small adjustment or correction of the printing plate, often shows on subsequent stamps printed from the plate.

- **Revenue Stamps:** Stamps issued for use on various taxable articles (playing cards, tobacco, wines, documents, patented medicines, stock certificates, mortgages, etc.) to show that the required government tax has been paid.

- **Reversed:** A left/right mirror image (usually refers to the watermark).

- **R.H.:** Receiving House.

- **R.L.B.:** Returned Letter Branch.

- **R.L.S.:** Returned Letter Section.

- **R.M.S.:** Railway Mail Sorter.

- **Rocket Mail:** Mail flown in a rocket, even if only a short distance. Many rocket mail experiments have been conducted since 1931. Special labels, cachets or cancels usually note that mail was carried on a rocket.

- **Roll:** The coil of stamp.

- **Rotary Press Printing:** Printing of stamps made from curved plates on a rotary press instead of flat plates on a flat-bed press. When plates are curved from a rotary press, they stretch slightly, and therefore, produce stamp designs slightly wider or higher than the identical designs printed from flat plates.

- **Roulette:** A tool or machine with a revolving toothed wheel used in engraving or making slit-shaped perforations between postage stamps.

- **R.P.O.:** Railway Post Office.

- **R.S.O.:** Railway Sorting or Sub-office. Sometimes, the nearest P.O. to railway track.

- **Rub:** Surface damaged due to cut, deletion of a cancel, or other unwanted mark.

- **Run:** Faded colour due to fugitive ink becoming damp.

- **Rural Free Delivery (R.F.D.):** System for free home delivery of mail in rural areas of the United States, begun just prior to the turn of the 20th century.

- **Rust:** A brown mold resembling the rust in iron. Rust affects stamp paper and gum in tropical regions.

(S)

- **S:** Scarce; Specimen.

- **S.C.:** Sorting Carriage.

- **Schiffspost:** Ship post.

- **Selvedge:** The gummed, stitched, or stapled margin of a booklet pane is usually left in the discarded booklet after the pane has been used.

- **Self-Adhesive:** Stamp gum that adheres to envelope paper by the application of pressure alone. Most self-adhesive stamps are sold on a coated paper release liner. See also Liner, Linerless, Water-activated.

- **Semi-Postal Stamps:** A special type of stamp made by various governments to be used for postage, as well as a means of obtaining funds for some deserving charity. The extra charge, which goes to the charity, is inscribed or overprinted on the stamp and must be paid by the person buying the stamp.

- **Series:** A number of postage stamps of different designs or denominations issued together or over a fairly short period to serve as a related group.

- **Service Inscribed:** A stamp with wording as part of the initial printed design that identifies the mail-handling service for which the stamp is intended, such as "Pre-sorted First-Class".

- **Set:** A number of stamps belonging to a particular issue or series. A complete set includes all the stamps of the series. An incomplete or broken set includes some, but not all of the stamps. When the denominations of an incomplete set are consecutive or incomplete as far as they go but stop short of the higher values, the set is called a Short Set.

- **Se-Tenant:** Joined together; a term applied to two or more un-separated stamps having different values, overprint or design, and printed that way intentionally, not through an error.

- **Shade:** A precise colour of ink used to print a postage stamp or part of its design. Several stamps, apparently printed in one colour, are catalogued in as many as eighteen shades.

- **Sheet:** A complete unit of stamps as printed. Stamps are usually printed in large sheets and are separated into two or more panes before shipment to post offices.

- **Shift:** A postage stamp printed in more than one colour in which one colour is noticeably off-centre.

- **Ship Letter: An** early letter carried by a private ship in charge of the captain and franked as a ship letter when handed over to the post office at the port of arrival. The handstamp is applied to a letter arriving by ship.

- **Short Perf.:** Postage stamp in which one of the teeth around its edge has been shortened or torn off, either in separating it from its neighbour or subsequently.

- **Short Set:** A set of postage stamps in which the top value is missing or in which the most 'difficult' value is missing).

- **Short Stamp:** Postage stamp in which the top and the bottom edges are closer together than usual, as a result of the method of operation of the perforating machine. The top row is one hole shorter than the remainder in nearly all early British perforated stamps.

- **S.F.:** Space Filler, with significant defects.

- **S.G.:** Stanley Gibbons.

- **Side:** Abbreviation for sideways watermark.

- **Side Delivery:** Coil machine dispensing a roll of side-by-side postage stamps.

- **Single:** Individual postage stamp.

- **Sleeper:** Stamp or other collectible item that seems to be underpriced and may have good investment potential.

- **Soaking:** Removal of stamps from envelope paper. Most stamps may be safely soaked in water. However, fugitive inks will run in water, and chalky-surfaced papers will lose their designs entirely, so some knowledge of stamps is a necessity. Coloured envelope paper should be soaked separately.

- **Soldier's Letter:** The term applied to a letter posted by a serving soldier, carried at a reduced rate.

- **Souvenir Card:** A philatelic card, not valid for postage, issued in conjunction with some special event. The souvenir card often illustrates the design of a postage stamp.

- **Souvenir Sheet:** A variety of "Miniature Sheet" issued by a country in honour or commemoration of some person, occasion or event. The margins then carry an inscription designating the purpose of the issue.

- **Space-Filler:** A stamp which is not of high quality, used to fill a space in an album where one of high quality is difficult to obtain.

- **Special Printing:** Reissue of a stamp of current or recent design, often with distinctive colour, paper or perforations.

- **Special Stamps:** Regular postage stamp issues that fall outside the traditional definitions of commemorative and definitive stamps. In the United States, holiday issues such as Contemporary Christmas, Traditional Christmas, Hanukkah and the like are considered special stamps. They are printed in substantially greater quantities than commemorative stamps, and sometimes return to press for additional printings. Love stamps are also considered special stamps.

- **Specimen:** A stamp used as an example and overprinted as such.

- **Speculative Issue:** A stamp or issue released primarily for sale to collectors rather than to meet any legitimate postal need.

- **Splice:** Repairing a break in a roll of stamp paper, or joining two rolls of paper for continuous printing. Stamps printed over a splice are usually removed and destroyed before the normal stamps are issued.

- **Spoon:** A duplex cancellation, the left half of which was usually oval in shape, somewhat resembling a spoon.

- **Squared-Circle:** A circular date handstamp contained within a square.

- **Stamps:** A small adhesive piece of paper stuck to something to show that an amount of money has been paid, in particular a postage stamp.

- **Stamp Money:** Unused postage stamps used as coins during shortages.

- **Stampless Covers:** Envelopes or sheets folded into envelope form with the written message on the inside, which were sent through the mail in the early days before stamps came into use.

- **Stated-to-catalogue:** If an auctioneer has a lot consisting of a large number of stamps, he may take the vendor's word for the catalogue value without checking it.

- **Stock Book:** A specially manufactured blank book containing rows of pockets on each page to hold stamps.

- **Strike:** The quality of the impression of a handstamp or cancel is described as 'a fine strike' or 'blurred strike', etc.

- **Strip:** Three or more unused postage stamps from the same row.

- **S.O.:** Sorting Office.

- **S.T.:** Sorting Tender-on.

- **S.T.C.:** Stated To Catalogue. The term used by auctioneers for lots where the vendor has calculated the Catalogue value. The auctioneer does not bear any responsibility for this statement.

- **Straight Edge:** A stamp issued with one or two adjacent sides without perforations caused by cutting a sheet into panes.

- **Surcharge (Sur):** An overprinted revaluation of a stamp, which usually includes blocking out the original denomination (face value).

(T)

- **T:** Tax or Underpaid mail.

- **Tagging:** Phosphor material on stamps used to activate automatic mail-handling equipment. This may be lines, bars, letters, part of the design area or the entire stamp surface. The tagging may also permeate the stamp paper. Some stamps are issued both with and without tagging. Catalogs describe them as tagged or untagged.

- **Tax Stamp:** Issued to raise funds (compulsory use).

- **Telegraph Cancel:** Cancellation, usually a small cds showing that the postage stamp was used on a telegram despatch form.

- **Telegraph Stamps:** Stamps used for the payment of a telegram service.

- **Testing Label:** A stamp-sized label used for testing automatic stamp vending machines.

- **Tele-Beche:** Two adjoining stamps with one being upside down in relation to the other.

- **Thematic:** The collecting of stamps according to a theme. E.g. Aircraft, Birds, Cricket, Disney, Explorers, Football, Ships, Writers, etc.

- **Thin:** A thin is an area where part of the back of a postage stamp has been torn away by clumsy removal from a cover or album page.

- **Tied:** A term used when a stamp is cancelled with a postmark straddles both the stamp and cover.

- **Tone Spot:** A mark on a stamp of brown rusty appearance which detracts from its value.

- **Tongs or Stamp Tongs:** Metal tweezers with which stamps can be handled rapidly and without soiling them.

- **Too Late:** A handstamp applied to a letter to indicate that it had been posted too late for inclusion in the day's dispatch.

- **Town Penny Post:** A local post; one penny is charged for letters delivered within its surroundings.

- **Town Stamp:** A handstamp usually containing the name of a town alone.

- **T.P.O.:** Travelling Post Office (A mail train in which the post is sorted and cancelled with TPO marks.

- **Training Stamp:** Postage stamp identical in most respects to current postage stamps but grossly altered to render it invalid for postage (usually by crude black overprint bars) and used to train new counter clerks.

- **Transit Strike:** A handstamp applied during the transit of a letter between the offices of posting and destination.

- **Typo Graphed:** Printed from type or from printing places on which the design is raised above the level of the plate (as distinguished from engraved plates where the design is cut into the flat surfaces of the metal).

(U)

- **U:** Used.

- **U/M:** Abbreviation for Unmounted Mint, never hinged.

- **Universal Postal Union (U.P.U.):** An international organisation formed in 1874, of which virtually all countries are members.

- **Un:** Unused.

- **Uncat:** Uncatalogued.

- **Uncatalogued:** This usually means it is known to exist and is listed in the catalogue but unpriced.

- **Under Print:** Inscription on the back of a postage stamp, usually under the gum and in the same ink used to print the front. Some underprints are 'protective'; they state the name or initials of the organisation which bought the stamp and which may use it. Other underprints are advertisements or fine geometric patterns serving a protective function.

- **Ungummed:** A stamp without gum. Ungummed stamps are either issued without gum or an un-canceled gummed stamp that has had its gum soaked. Many countries in tropical climates have issued stamps without gum.

- **Unhinged:** A stamp without hinge marks, but not necessarily with original gum.

- **Uniform Four-Penny Post:** From 5th December 1839 to 9th January 1840, letters posted were charged a uniform postage rate of 4d instead of postage calculated by distance.

- **Uniform Penny Post:** From 10th January 1840, letters posted within the United Kingdom were charged a uniform postage rate if 1d.

- **Unissued:** Adhesive stamps prepared for use but not issued.

- **Un-Perforated:** Imperforate or the stamps without perforation.

- **Unsorted:** Applies to an accumulation or loose mixture (e.g. kiloware), which means that nobody has inspected the stamps to see if anything of value is present; thus, the mass may contain a rarity.

- **Unused:** The stamp that has not been cancelled but is not necessarily a mint stamp.

- **Used:** The term applied to a stamp that has been through the postal system. Categories of used are Superb Used, Fine Used, Good Used, and Used.

- **Used Abroad:** Where stamps from one country are used and cancelled in another. Quite common in cases such as British Colonies or Possessions. Spain and France were also countries that issued stamps that were used in other countries of the world over which they had influence. These stamps can only be distinguished by the postmark applied.

- **Un-Watermarked (U.W.):** Not watermarked; a term applied to a stamp that is printed on un-watermarked paper.

- **U.V.:** Ultra-Violet light.

(V)

- **V, VV, VVV:** Symbols used to indicate 'valuable' to 'extremely valuable'.

- **Value:** Face value, when referring to the amount of money for which the stamp was sold at a post office and for which postal service will be rendered. Monetary or market value, when referring to its worth as a philatelic commodity.

- **Variety:** A stamp which has a flaw or error.

- **Veld Post:** Field Post.

- **Vignette:** The central part of a stamp design.

(W)

- **Want List:** A list of needed stamps or covers, identified by catalog number or some other description, submitted by a collector to a dealer, usually including requirements on condition and price.

- **War Stamp:** A stamp which is issued in time of war to raise additional revenue and inscribed **War Stamp** or **War Tax** or such similar words.

- **Water Activated Adhesive:** Stamp gum designed to adhere to envelope paper only if the gum is moistened. All gummed stamps before 1963 used water-activated adhesive.

- **Watermark:** A design, character, letters, numerals or words impressed into paper during the manufacturing process and visible in part or whole in each stamp printed on such paper.

- **Watermark Detector:** A flat black tray or surface used in seeing or "detecting" the watermark on a stamp. The stamp is laid face down on the tray, moistened with a few drops of special fluid, and the watermark usually shows quite clearly.

- **Weak:** Portion of a postage stamp that, though imperfect, is not bad enough to be described as damaged, particularly applied to corners, which may be slightly thinned or shortened.

- **Web:** A continuous roll of paper used in stamp printing.

- **Wilding:** A definitive stamp of Great Britain which was issued in the 1950s-1960s and designed by Dorothy Wilding.

- **Wing Margin:** Postage stamps from sheets divided by wide gutters into panes may have a wing margin along one side, there being a wide imperforate margin between the printed design and the perforation.

- **Window Booklet:** A booklet of stamps which originally revealed the stamps inside through a cut in the cover of the booklet.

- **Wove Paper:** General term for a range of papers produced by settling fibres on fine wire mesh which imprints a watermark, giving a woven appearance.

- **Wreak Mail:** Mail carried on ships or aircraft that were wrecked or torpedoed. It has been the custom of the Post office to put special marks on the recovered mail to explain the damage.

(Z)

- **Zemstvo:** A local stamp issued by Russian municipal governments in accordance with an imperial edict of 1870.

- **Zeppelins:** The stamps issued for, or in honour of, zeppelin flights. Cacheted covers carried on such flights are Zeppelin covers.

- **ZIP Block:** U.S. marginal marking block with the selvage bearing the image of the "Mr. ZIP" cartoon character and/or an inscription urging the use of a ZIP code. This first appeared on U.S. marginal selvage in 1964. Typically, a ZIP block is a block of four stamps.

- **ZIP Code:** Numerical postcode used to speed and mechanize handling and delivery. The letters stand for "Zoning Improvement Plan".

10

Stamp Recognizing

A Guide To Identifying Stamps

The names mentioned on the stamps of some countries might differ from the actual name of the country due to colonial references, local languages, and territorial shifts over time, making it challenging for collectors to identify stamps issued by those countries accurately.

Below is a list of such countries (in alphabetical order) whose names on the stamp differ from the name of the country, making it easier for collectors to recognize.

Name Printed on Stamp	Actual Name of The Country

A

Name Printed on Stamp	Actual Name of The Country
A. & T. (Overprint)	Annan & Tonquin (Indo-China)
A.B. (Overprint)	Far Eastern Republic (Russia)
Acores	Azores (Portuguese Colonies)
Afghanes	Afghanistan
Africa Correios	Portuguese Colony in Africa
Africa Occidental Espanola	Spanish Western Sahara (Spanish Colony)
Africa Orientale Italiane	Italian East Africa (Italian Colony)
Afrique Equatoriale Francaise	French Equatorial Africa (French Colony)
Afrique Occidentale Francaise	French West Africa (French Colony)

Name Printed on Stamp	Actual Name of The Country
Alexendrie (Overprint)	French Post office in Egypt (France)
Allemagne Duitschland (Overprint)	Germany
Algerie	Algeria
AMGFIT (Overprint)	Trieste (Italy)
AMGVG (Overprint)	Venezia Giulia (Italy)
Annas	British Post office in Persian Gulf
Antillen	Antilles (Dutch Colony)
A Payer Te Betalen	Belgium (Postage Due)
Arabie Saoudite	Saudi Arabia
Archipel Des Comores	Comoro Islands
Avisporto Maerke	Denmark
Ayuntamiento De Barcelona	Barcelona (Spain)

B

B. A. Eritrea (Overprint)	Eritrea (British Post office)
B. A. Somalia (Overprint)	Somalia (British Post office)
B. A. Tripolitania (Overprint)	Tripolitania (British Post office)
Bajar Porto	Indonesia (Postage Due)
Bani	Romania
Bayern	Bavaria (Germany)

Name Printed on Stamp	Actual Name of The Country
B. C. A. (Overprint)	British Central Africa (Nyasaland)
Belgien (Overprint)	Belgium
Belgique	Belgium
Benadir	Italian Somaliland
Bengasi (Overprint)	Italian Levant (Italy)
Beyrouth (Overprint)	Russian Levant (Russia)
B.M.A. (Overprint)	Malaya
Bohmen U. Mahren	Bohemia and Moravia (Czechoslovakia)
Bosnien	Bosnia (Yugoslavia)
Braunschweig	Brunswick (German State)
British Central Africa	Nyasaland
British New Guinea	Papua
British South Africa (Company)	Rhodesia
Buu Chinh	Vietnami word for post

C

Name Printed on Stamp	Actual Name of The Country
Cabo Juby	Cape Juby (Spanish Colony)
Cabo Verde	Cape Varde Islands
Calchi (Overprint)	Aegean Islands (Italy)
Calimno (Overprint)	Aegean Islands (Italy)
Calino (Overprint)	Aegean Islands (Italy)
Castelrosso (Overprint)	Aegean Islands (Italy)

Name Printed on Stamp	Actual Name of The Country
Cavalle (Overprint)	French Levant (France)
Caso (Overprint)	Aegean Islands (Italy)
C. C. C. P.	Russia
C. CH.	French Cochin China (Indo-China)
C.E.F.(On Cameroun stamps)	British Cameroons
C.E.F. (On Indian stamps)	India
Centisimi	Italy
Centimose	French Morocco (currency)
Centrafrica	Central Africa
Ceskoslovensko	Czechoslovakia
Ceskych	Czechoslovakia
C. F. A. (Overprint)	Reunion
C. G. H. S. (Overprint)	Upper Silesia (Germany)
Cilicie (Overprint)	Cilicia (Turkey)
Co. CI. (Overprint)	Slovenia (Yugoslavia)
Coamo	Puerto Rico
Commission Interalliee Marenwerder	Marienwerder (Germany)
Companhia De Mocambique	Mozambique Company
Comunicacions	Spain (Post)
Congo Belge	Belgian Congo
Congo Francais Gabon	Gabon

Name Printed on Stamp	Actual Name of The Country
Constantinople (Overprint)	Russian Levant (Russia)
Constantinopoli (Overprint)	Italian Post office in Turkey
COO (Overprint)	Aegean Islands (Italy)
Coree	Korea
Correio	Portugal
Correio India	Portuguese India
Correspondencia Urgente (Overprint)	Express Delivery (Spain)
Cos (Overprint)	Aegean Islands (Italy)
Cote D' Ivoire	Ivory Coast
Cote Francaise Des Somalio	French Somali Coast

D

Name Printed on Stamp	Actual Name of The Country
Dai Nippon (Overprint)	Malaya
Dan Chu Cong Hoa	North Vietnam (Vietnam)
Dansk Vestindi (SK) E (N)	Danish West Indies
D D R	East Germany
Dedeagh (Overprint)	French Levant (France)
Dell'egeo (Overprint)	Aegean Islands (Italy)
Deutsche Bundapost	West Germany
Deutsche Luftpost	Germany
Deutsche Post	Germany
Deutsche Post Berlin	West Berlin (Germany)

Name Printed on Stamp	Actual Name of The Country
Deutsches Reich	Germany
Deutschösterreich	Austria
Deutsch Ostrfrica	German East Africa
Deutsch Post Osten (Overprint)	Poland
Deutsch-Sudwest Africa	South-West Africa
DJ (Overprint)	Djibouti (French Somali coast)
Doplata	Postage Due (Several countries of East Europe)
DRZAVA S.H.S. (Overprint)	Yugoslavia
Durazzo (Overprint)	Italian Post office (Italy)

E

Name Printed on Stamp	Actual Name of The Country
E.A. F. (Overprint)	British Post office
E. E. F.	Palestine
Eesti	Estonia
EGEO (Overprint)	Aegean Islands (Italy)
Eire	Ireland
Elsaß (Overprint)	Alsace (Germany)
Escuelas	Venezuela
Espana	Spain
Espanola	Spain
Estado Da Guine-Bissau	Guinea Bissau
Estado Da India	Portuguese India

Name Printed on Stamp	Actual Name of The Country
Estada Espanol	Spain
Estero (Overprint)	Italian Post office in Turkey
Establishments Dans L'Inde	French India
Etablissements De L'Oceanie	Oceanic Settlements (French Colony)
Etat Independent Du Congo	Belgian Congo
Eithiopie	Abyssinia (Ethiopia)
Eithiopiennes	Abyssinia (Ethiopia)
Ets Francs De L' Oceania	Oceanic Settlements (French Colony)
Eupen	Belgium

F

Filipinas	Philippine Islands
Fivme	Fiume
Foroyar	Faroe Islands
Francaise	France
Francaise De L'Oceanie	Oceanic Settlements (French Colony)
Franco	Switzerland (Currency)
Franco Bollo Postale	Papal States (Italy)
Freistaat Bayern (Overprint)	Bavaria (Germany)
Frimarke	Sweden

Name Printed on Stamp	Actual Name of The Country
G	
GAB (Overprint)	Gabon (French Colony)
Gabonaise	Gabon (French Colony)
G&D (Overprint)	Guadeloupe (French Colony)
Gdansk	Poland
GD. Liban	Lebanon
G. F.A. (Overprint)	Tanzania
General Government	Poland (Germany Occupation 193/45)
Gen. Gour. Warschau	Poland
Georgeinne	Georgia
Gerusalemme (Overprint)	Italian Post office in Turkey
G. K. C. A. (Overprint)	Carinthia (Austria)
Golfe De Benin	Benin
Golfo De Guinea	Spanish Guinea
G.P.E. (Overprint)	Guadeloupe (French Colony)
Grande Comore	Grand Comoro (Malagasy)
Grand Liban	Lebanon
G.R.I. (Overprint)	Samoa (British Occupation)
Gronland	Greenland
Grossdeutsches Reich	Germany
G. R. Post Mafia (Overprint)	Tanzania

Name Printed on Stamp	Actual Name of The Country
Guine	Portuguese Guinea
Guinea Continental (Overprint)	Spanish Guinea
Guinea Francaise	French Guinea
Guinea Espanola	Spanish Guinea
Gültig 9. Armee (Overprint)	Germany
Guyane Francaise	French Guyana

H

Name Printed on Stamp	Actual Name of The Country
Hatay Devlet	Hatay (Turkey)
Haute Silesia	Upper Silesia
Haute Volta	Upper Volta
Haut-Senegal Niger	Upper Senegal & Niger
H. E. H. The Nizam's Govt.	Hyderabad
H. H. Nawab Shahjahan Begum	Bhopal
Helvetia	Switzerland
Herzegowina	Bosnia & Herzegovina (Yugoslavia)
Holkar	Indore
HRVATSKA	Croatia (Yugoslavia)
HRVATSKA SHS	State of Slovenes, Croats and Serbs
HT. SENEGAL-NIGER	Upper Senegal & Niger

Name Printed on Stamp	Actual Name of The Country

I

Name Printed on Stamp	Actual Name of The Country
I. E. F. (Overprint)	India
I. E. F. 'D' (Overprint)	Mosul (Iraq)
Ierusalem (Overprint)	Russian Levant (Russia)
ILE Rouad	French Levant (France)
Imperio Colonial Portuguese	Portuguese Colony in Africa
Imprime	Turkey
India Port	Portuguese India
Inkeri	Ingria (Finland)
Ionikon Kpatoe	Ionian Islands
Iran	Persia (Iran)
Iranennes	Persia (Iran)
Isole Italiane Dell'egeo (Overprint)	Aegean Islands (Italy)
Island	Iceland
Italiane/no	Italy
Italiane Isol Dell' egeo	Aegean Islands (Italy)

J

Name Printed on Stamp	Actual Name of The Country
Jaffa (Overprint)	Russian Levant (Russia)
Janina (Overprint)	Italy
Java (Overprint)	Indonesia
Jugoslavija	Yugoslavia

Name Printed on Stamp	Actual Name of The Country

K

Name Printed on Stamp	Actual Name of The Country
Kamerun	Camerouns
Kampuchea	Cambodia
Karki (Overprint)	Aegean Islands (Italy)
Karnten Abstimmung (Overprint)	Carinthia (Austria)
Karolinen	Caroline Islands
Kathiri State of Seiyun	Seiyun (State of Aden)
Kerassunde (Overprint)	Russian Levant (Russia)
KGL. Post FRM	Denmark
Klaipeda	Lithuania
KNTAN (Overprint)	Russian China
KPHTH	Crete
Kraljivstvo SHS	Yugoslavia
K. U. K. FIELD POST	Austria
K. U. K. MILITAR POST	Austria
K. WÜRTT. POST	Württemberg (Germany)

L

Name Printed on Stamp	Actual Name of The Country
La CANEA (Overprint)	Italy
La Georgia	Georgia
LAND-POST PORTO-MARKE	Baden (Germany)
LATTAQUIE (Overprint)	Syria
Latvija	Latvia

Name Printed on Stamp	Actual Name of The Country
Latwija	Latvia
Leros (Overprint)	Aegean Islands (Italy)
Liban	Lebanon
Libanaise	Lebanon
Lietuva	Lithonia
Lietuvos	Lithonia
Lipso (Overprint)	Aegean Islands (Italy)
Lisso (Overprint)	Aegean Islands (Italy)
Litwa Strodkowa	Central Lithonia
Losen	Sweden (Postage Due)
Lothringen (Overprint)	Lorraine (France)
LUEBECK	Lubeck (German State)
Lubiana (Overprint)	Slovenia (Yugoslavia)

M

MACAV	Macao
Magyar	Hungary
Msgyarkir	Hungary
Magyarorszag	Hungary
Malgache	Malagasy
Malmedy (Overprint)	Germany
Marianas Espanolas (Overprint)	Marianne Islands (Spanish Colony)
Marianen	Marianne Islands (German Colony)

Name Printed on Stamp	Actual Name of The Country
Marki	Finland (Currency)
Maroc	French Morocco
Marreucos	Spanish Morocco
Marshall Inseln	Marshall Islands (German State)
Medolin	Medellin (Columbia)
M. E. F. (Overprint)	Middle East Forces (British Post office)
Mejico	Mexico
Memel-Gebiet (Overprint)	Memel (Lithonia)
Metelin (Overprint)	Russian Levant
Militar Post	Bosnia (Yugoslavia)
Mocambique	Mozambique
Modonesi	Modena (Italy)
Mongtze	Mong Tseu (Indo China)
Mont-Athos (Overprint)	Russian Levant
Montevideo	Uruguay
Moyen Congo	Central Congo
MQE (Overprint)	Martinique (French Colony)
M.V.I. R. (Overprint)	Romania

Name Printed on Stamp	Actual Name of The Country

N

Name Printed on Stamp	Actual Name of The Country
Napoletana	Naples (Italy)
Nations Unies	U.N.O.
Nations Unies Office Europeon	U.N.O.
NCE	New Caledonia
Nederland	Holland
Ned Indie	Dutch Indies (Indonesia)
Nederlandsch Indie	Dutch Indies (Indonesia)
N. F. (Overprint)	Tanzania
Nieuwe Republiek	New Republic (West Africa)
Nieuw Guinea	Dutch New Guinea (Dutch Colony)
Nisiro (Overprint)	Aegean Islands (Italy)
Nlle Caledonie	New Caledonia
Norddeutscher	German States
Norge	Norway
Nouvelle Caledonie	New Caledonia
Nouvelle Hebrides	New Hebrides (French Colony)
Noyta	Russia
Nippon	Japan
NSB (Overprint)	Nosy-Be (Malagasy)
N. Sembilan	Negeri Sembilan

Name Printed on Stamp	Actual Name of The Country
NSW	New South Wales
N. W. Pacific Islands (Overprint)	New Guinea

O

Name Printed on Stamp	Actual Name of The Country
Oesterr	Austria
Oesterreich	Austria
Offentlig Sak	Norway
OKCA	Russia
OLTRE GIUBA	Jubaland (Italian Colony)
O. M. F. Cilicie (Overprint)	Cilicia (Turkey)
O. M. F. Syrie (Overprint)	Syria
Oranje Vrij Staat	Orange Free State
Oriental	Uruguay
Osterreich	Austria
Ostland (Overprint)	Germany (Military)
Ottomanes	Turkey
Oubanbui-chari	Ubangi Shari (French Colony)

P

Name Printed on Stamp	Actual Name of The Country
Pacchi Postali	Italy or San Marino (Parcel Post)
Para	Currency of Yugoslavia & Turkey
Paras (Overprint)	Foreign P.O. in Turkey

Name Printed on Stamp	Actual Name of The Country
Patmos (Overprint)	Aegean Islands (Italy)
PC-CP	Russia
PE	Egypt
Pechino (Overprint)	Italy
Penni	Finland (Currency)
Persanes	Persia (Iran)
Pesa	German East Africa
Peseta (Overprint)	French Morocco
P. G. S. (Overprint)	Perak (Malaya)
Piastre (Overprint)	Foreign Post office in Turkey
Pilipinas	Philippine Islands
Piscopi	Aegean Islands (Italy)
Poccir	Russia
Polska	Poland
Polynesia Francaise	French Polynesia
Porteado	Portugal (postage Due)
Port Lagos (Overprint)	French Levant
Port Gdansk	Danzig (Poland Post office)
Postes Eqyptiennes	Egypt
Postas Le N'ioc	Ireland
Postes	Postage (French Word)
Poste Italian Rodi	Aegean Islands (Italy)

Name Printed on Stamp	Actual Name of The Country
Post Stamp, Postage or Post & Receipt	Hyderabad
Postzegel	Holland
Preussen	Prussia (German State)
Provinz Laibach	Slovenia (Yugoslavia)
Provinz Sachsen	Saxony (German States)
Pto-Rico	Puerto Rico (Spanish Colony)
Puttialla (Overprint)	Patiala (Indian State)

Q

Quaiti State in Hadhramaut	Hadhramaut (Aden State)
Quaiti State in Shihr and Mukalla	Hadhramaut (Aden State)

R

R (Overprint)	Reunion
Rarotonga	Cook Islands
Rialtas Sealadach na hÉireann	Ireland
Regno D'Italia Venegia Giulia (Overprint)	Austria
REICHPOST	Germany
REPVBLICA PORTVGVESA	Portugal
Republica, Republique	Word for Republic
R. F.	France

Name Printed on Stamp	Actual Name of The Country
Rizeh (Overprint)	Russian Levant
R. O. (Overprint)	Eastern Rumelia (Turkey)
Rodi (Overprint)	Aegean Islands (Italy)
Romana	Romania
Roumelie Orientale	Eastern Rumelia (Turkey)
Royaume De L' Arabie Soudite	Saudi Arabia
Royaume Du Laos	Laos
Royarnme Du Maroc	Morocco
R. S. M. (Overprint)	San Marino

S

Saargebiet	Saar (German States)
Sachson	Saxony (German States)
Sahara Espanol	Spanish Sahara
Salonicco (Overprint)	Italy
Salonique (Overprint)	Russian Levant
Samoa I Sisifo	Samoa
Sandiak D' Alexandrette	Hatay (Turkey)
Sarkari	Saurashtra (Service)
Scarpanto (Overprint)	Aegean Islands (Italy)
Scutari di Albania (Overprint)	Italian Post office in Albania
Segnatasse Sen	Currency in Japan
Serbien	Serbia (Yugoslavia)

Name Printed on Stamp	Actual Name of The Country
Shquipenie	Albania
Shqiperia	Albania
Shqipni	Albania
Shqiptare	Albania
S. H. S. (Overprint)	Yugoslavia
Siam	Thailand
Simi (Overprint)	Aegean Islands (Italy)
Slosvig	Schleswig (Denmark)
Slovenska	Slovakia
Smirne (Overprint)	Italian Post office in Turkey
Smyrne (Overprint)	Russian Levant
SO	East Silesia (Poland)
Sociote Des Nations (Overprint)	League of Nations
Soudan Francais	French Sudan
South Africa Company	Rhodesia
Sowjetische Besatzungs Zone (Overprint)	Germany (Russian occupation)
S. P. M. (Overprint)	St. Pierre P. Miquelon
Srba Hrvata Slovenaca	Yugoslavia
Srodkowa Litwa	Central Lithonia
Stadt Berlin	Berlin (Germany)
Stampalia	Aegean Islands (Italy)
Stati Parm (Overprint)	Parma (Italy)

Name Printed on Stamp	Actual Name of The Country
Stati Parmensi (Overprint)	Parma (Italy)
S. Thomas	St. Thomas & Prince Is.
S. Thomas E Principe	St. Thomas & Prince Is.
Straits Settlements	Malaya
STT. Vuja	Trieste (Italy)
Suid Africa	South Africa
Sultanat D' Anjouan	Anjouan (Malagasy)
S. Ujong	Sungei Ujong (Malaya)
Soumi	Finland
Sverige	Sweden (Postage Due)
Syrienne	Syria

T

Name Printed on Stamp	Actual Name of The Country
Tanger (Overprint)	French Morocco
Tanger	Tangier
Tchad	Tchad (French Colony)
Te Betalen	Belgium (Postage Due)
Te Betalen Post	Holland (Postage Due)
T. E. O. (Overprint)	Syria
T. E. O. Cilicia (Overprint)	Cilicia (Turkey)
Terres Australes Et Antarctigue Francaises	French South & Antarctic Country
Territoire De L'ININI	Inini (French Colony)
Territoise Du Niger	Niger
Tetuan (Overprint)	Spanish Morocco

Name Printed on Stamp	Actual Name of The Country
Thai	Thailand (Siam)
Thailand	Thailand (Siam)
Thuringen	Thuringia (German States)
Tientsin (Overprint)	Italian Post office in China
Timbre Movil	Spain
Tienestafrimerke	Norway
Toga	Tonga
Togolaise	Togo
To Pay	Great Britain (Postage Due)
Trebizonde (Overprint)	Russian Levant
Trentino (Overprint)	Austria
Tridentina (Overprint)	Austria
Tunisie	Tunisia
Turkiye	Turkey

U

U.A.E.	United Arab Emirates
U. A. R.	Egypt
Ultramar	Cuba
U. S.	U. S. A.

V

Valona (Overprint)	Italian Post office in Albania
Van Diemens Land	Tasmania
Vanthy (Overprint)	French Levant

Name Printed on Stamp	Actual Name of The Country
Venezia Giulia (Overprint)	Austria
Vietnam Cong Hoa	South Vietnam
Vojenska Posta	Siberia (Czechoslovakia)
Vojna Uprava Jugoslavenske Armije	Istria (Yugoslavia)
Vrvgvay	Uruguay

W

Wallis Et Futuna	Wallis & Futuna

Y

Y. A. R.	Yemen
YCCP	Ukraine (Russia)

Z

Ziud Afrikaansche Republiek	Transvaal
Zeitungs	Austria
Zone Francaise	French Part of Germany
Zuid West Africa	South West Africa

11

Global Renaming

Countries That Have Altered Their Names Due to Various Factors

Several countries in the world have changed their names over the years due to various reasons such as political changes, independence movements, or rebranding efforts. Here is a list of some countries that have changed their names:

Old Name	New Name
Aden	Southern Yemen
Afars & Issas	Djibouti
Basutoland	Lesetho
Bechuanaland	Botswana
Belgian Congo	Zaire
British Honduras	Belize
Burma	Myanmar
Ceylon	Sri Lanka
Czechoslovakia	Czech Republic & Slovakia
Dahomey	Benin
Ellics Is.	Tuvalu
Gilbert Is	Kiribati
Gold Coast	Ghana
Kampuchea	Cambodia
Madagascar	Malagasy
Netherlands Indies	Indonesia
New Hebridges	Vanuatu
Northern Rhodesia	Zambia
Nyasaland	Malawi
Portuguese Guinea	Guinea Bissau

Old Name	New Name
Siam	Thailand
South West Africa	Namibia
Southern Rhodesia	Zimbabwe
Swaziland	Eswatini
Upper Volta	Burkina Faso
Yugoslav Republic of Macedonia	North Macedonia

12

The Stamp Quiz

Testing Your Knowledge of Philately and Stamps

General Questions

1. Which country issued the first postage stamp of the world, and in which year?

2. What was the first adhesive Postage stamp issued?

3. When were the first postage stamps issued in India? In which part of the country they were issued?

4. In which year were the first postage stamps issued to be used in whole India?

5. After independence, the first stamp of India was issued on what topic and on what date?

6. Which country issued the world's first bicolour stamp?

7. Which was the first country in the world to send the mail by air, and in which year?

8. Which stamp of India was printed in Switzerland?

9. India issued a set of stamps on Mahatma Gandhi in 1948. What are the denominations?

10. On which commemorative stamps of India the word "SERVICE" was overprinted?

11. Before independence, who was the King of Great Britain whose stamps were printed in India?

12. In which year was the first postage stamp issued on Golden Temple in India?

13. In which year was the first stamp issued on the Taj Mahal in India?

14. After independence, when was the first definite series issued in India, and what was the theme?

15. After independence, when was the second definite series issued in India, and what was the theme?

16. National Philatelic day is celebrated on?

17. World Post Day is celebrated on?

18. The headquarter of Universal Postal Union (UPU)?

19. Name the first Indian Newspaper to be honoured on Postal Stamp.

20. The only person in the wolrd to be honoured with a stamp over 43 countries of the globe?

21. The first foreigner to be honoured on Indian Stamp?

22. Which is the only country in the world that has no country name on its postage stamps?

23. Name the Country that has the largest postal network in the world.

24. Where was the first Post office opened in India in 1927?

25. Asia's first adhesive stamp, the Scinde Dawk, was introduced in which year?

26. When was the first General Post office opened in India?

27. The world's Highest Post office is located in?

28. What is the full form of PIN?

29. When was the Postal Index Number (PIN) introduced in India?

30. How many postal index number zones India has been divided into?

31. The headquarter of India Post is situated in?

32. Who was the first Indian King to be depicted on an Indian Stamp?

33. The National Philatelic Museum of India is situated in?

34. How many digits are there in the Postal Index Number (PIN) code of India?

35. What is the PIN code of the Supreme Court of India?

36. Which is the first Indian post office outside Indian Territory?

37. The post office established at Dakshin Gangotri is under which postal Division?

38. Where is the Postal Staff College situated in India?

39. Indian Postal Day is observed on?

40. In India, Speed post was introduced in the year?

41. What is the Project launched by the Department of Post in 2008 to upgrade post offices in urban and rural areas and improve services?

42. In which List of the Constitution of India are posts included?

43. The First Indian to appear on a Postal Stamp was?

44. The First Indian woman to appear on a Postal Stamp was?

45. Which American President is known as a philatelic stamp collecting President?

46. The first country other than India to release a stamp on Mahatma Gandhi?

47. Who was the first foreign woman to be honoured on Indian Postal Stamp?

48. The term "Philately" was first used by?

49. The First Indian Stamp on a living personality was issued in 1958. Name the personality.

50. The First Cine Actress portrayed on Indian Postage Stamps?

51. The official language of the Universal Postal Union is?

52. The theme of 2016 World Post Day is?

53. Which is the rarest stamp of India?

54. Which is the rarest stamp of India after independence?

55. Which is the rarest stamp of the world?

56. What is the term for the small horizontal and vertical cuts between stamps to facilitate separation?

57. If there are no perforations (holes) in Stamps to separate them from the sheet, what are such stamps called?

58. Which is the lowest denomination stamp of India ever issued?

59. Which is the first triangular stamp issued in India?

60. Name any 5 Indian Native States whose stamps mail was valid for whole India before independence.

61. What is the use of a Service stamp?

62. Name the stamps which were withdrawn from the sale due to poor printing quality.

63. Name the country other than India that issued the stamp on Rajiv Gandhi.

64. Name the country other than India that issued the stamp on Lal Bahadur Shastri.

65. Who introduced the postage stamp system?

66. Who was the famous stamp collector on whom a stamp is issued in India?

67. What do you understand by tete-beche?

68. Which were the first tete-beche stamps of India?

69. What is the meaning of se-tenant?

70. Name the first se-tenant stamp of India.

71. In which year India issued the first miniature sheet, and on what?

72. What do you understand by the first day cover?

73. What is the identity of the Mint stamp?

74. What types of stamps are called commemorative?

75. What type of stamps is called definitive stamps?

76. If 4 stamps of same type are joined together in a square shape, what are they called?

77. What are stamp collectors called?

78. Which Country in 1898 produced the first Christmas stamp?

79. Which country in 1964 produced the first self-adhesive stamp?

80. If you see Helvetia written on a stamp, where is it from?

81. What term is applied to stamps issued for general use?

82. Which country is famous for its Nobel Stamps?

83. Amongst Asian countries who first released stamps?

84. Which country issued the world's first sports stamps?

85. On which occasion world's first sports stamps was issued?

86. What is the term used to describe stamp collection?

87. Stamp collecting is called Philately. What does it mean?

88. Before Independence, which country's stamps were in use in Bangladesh?

89. Which country is associated with the famous "Red Collection"?

90. Which country issued a stamp which could play the national anthem on a record?

91. Which country issued stamps that smelt and tasted of chocolate in 2013?

92. Which country uses the abbreviation RSA on its stamps?

Questions Related to Sikkim

93. When was the postal system introduced in Sikkim, and by whom?

94. Where was the first Post office of Sikkim opened and in which year?

95. The oldest postal cancellation of Sikkim available is of which date?

96. What was the first thematic stamp of Sikkim released by India Post, and in which year?

97. In which year Changu Lake stamp was released by India Post?

98. Who started the Sikkim Rocket-mail Experiment, and in which year?

99. Name the places where the Sikkim Rocket-mail Experiment was conducted.

100. Which mountain is featured on the revenue stamp of Sikkim?

101. When was the first scheduled Helicopter Mail Service started in India?

102. When was the first philatelic exhibition of Sikkim held?

Answers to The Stamp Quiz

1. Great Britain, 1840
2. Penny Black
3. 1852, Sind Province
4. 1854
5. The Indian Flag and on 21.11.47
6. India in 1854 4A
7. India in 1911
8. 1948 Mahatma Gandhi set
9. 11/2a, 31/2a, 12a and ₹10
10. 1948Mahatma Gandhi Set
11. King George VI
12. 1935 Silver Jubilee set 31/2a
13. 1935 Silver Jubilee 21/2a
14. 1949 Archaeological
15. 1955, Five Year Plan
16. October 12
17. October 9
18. Bern, Switzerland
19. Times of India
20. Mahatma Gandhi
21. Henry Dunant
22. Great Britain
23. India
24. Kolkata
25. 1852
26. 1774 (Kolkata)
27. Hikkim, Himachal Pradesh
28. Postal Index Number
29. 15th August 1972
30. 9 (Nine)
31. New Delhi
32. Chandra Gupta Maurya
33. New Delhi
34. 6 (Six)
35. 110201
36. At Dakshin Gangotri, Antarctica
37. Goa Postal Division
38. Ghaziabad, Uttar Pradesh
39. October 10
40. 1986
41. Project Arrow
42. Union List
43. Mahatma Gandhi
44. Meera Bai
45. Franklin D. Roosevelt
46. United States of America
47. Annie Besant
48. Georges Herpin
49. Dhondo Keshav Karve
50. Nargis Dutt on 30th December 1993

<table>
<tr><td>

51. French

52. Innovation, Integration and Inclusion

53. 1854 4a Queen's Head is inverted

54. 1948 Mahatma Gandhi ₹10 Service Overprinted

55. British Guiana 1856

56. Perforations

57. Imperforated Stamps

58. 1956 Map Series 1 Naya Paisa

59. 1985 Mountain Road ₹2

60. Gwalior, Patiala, Jind, Nabha and Chamba.

61. They are used by Government offices.

62. Rajiv Gandhi, Begum Akhtar & Water Birds 4 value set

63. Bhutan

64. Hungary

65. Sir Ronald Hill

66. Jal Cooper

67. Pair of 2 stamps of same type joint in Different direction

68. King George V 1a

69. Stamp of more than one design joint together

70. 1974 Mathura Museum

</td><td>

71. 1973 INDIPEX

72. Special Cover issued on the first day of any stamps

73. 73. Stamp which has no post mark and if they are issued with gum on back, it should be in perfect condition

74. Any stamps commemorating special person or theme and issued printed only once

75. Repeatedly printed stamps for general public use

76. Block of 4

77. Philatelist

78. Canada

79. Sierre Leone

80. Switzerland

81. Definitive Stamp

82. Sweden

83. India

84. Greece

85. First Olympic Games

86. Philately

87. The Collection and study of Postage stamps

88. Pakistan

89. Great Britain

90. Bhutan

</td></tr>
</table>

91. Belgium	98. Stephen Smith & in 1934 - 35
92. South Africa	99. Gangtok, Ray, Saramsa, Singtam and Rangpo.
93. In 1888 by The Political officer of Sikkim John Claude White	100. Mt. Siniolchu
94. Dalapchand (1888)	101. 7th January 1988, in between Gangtok (Sikkim) and Bagdogra (West Bengal)
95. 3rd October 1888 (Experimental P.O. C-3)	102. 1982
96. Mt. Kanchenjunga (1955)	
97. 2006	

Final Thoughts

In the pages of this book, I have embarked on a fascinating journey through the captivating world of stamp collecting and philately. From the humble beginnings of the stamp collection to the intricate details of building a philatelic exhibit, I've explored the rich history and evolution of postal mail, essential accessories for stamp collecting, and the art of selecting philatelic materials. I've researched the world of stamps, learning to recognize their unique features and understand the global renaming of countries.

As I conclude my exploration, it is clear that stamp collecting is more than just a hobby; it is a passionate pursuit that connects us with history, culture, and the world at large. The chapters in this book have provided the tools and knowledge necessary to embark on your own stamp collection journey, and the Philatelic Dictionary has equipped you with the language to navigate this unique hobby.

In closing, the Stamp Quiz serves as a reminder that the learning and discovery in the world of philately are never-ending. There is always more to explore, more stamps to discover, and more stories to tell. As you continue your stamp-collecting journey, you will join a community of enthusiasts who share your passion for these small but significant pieces of history.

Stamp collecting is a voyage of discovery, a tribute to the art of design, and a celebration of the diversity of our world. So, as you set out to build your own collection and create your unique philatelic exhibits, remember that the world of postage stamps is a treasure trove of knowledge and a testament to the enduring beauty of printed history. Embrace it, enjoy it, and continue to expand your horizons in the world of stamps.

*** Happy Collecting! ***